VOODOO CHILD

THE ILLUSTRATED LEGEND of JIMI HENDRIX

CREATED & PRODUCED BY
Martin I. Green

ILLUSTRATED BY
Bill Sienkiewicz

PENGUIN
STUDIO

PENGUIN STUDIO
Published by the Penguin Group
Penguin Books USA Inc., 375 Hudson Street,
New York, New York 10014, U.S.A.
Penguin Books Ltd, 27 Wrights Lane,
London W8 5TZ, England
Penguin Books Australia Ltd, Ringwood,
Victoria, Australia
Penguin Books Canada Ltd, 10 Alcorn Avenue,
Toronto, Ontario, Canada M4V 3B2
Penguin Books (N.Z.) Ltd, 182–190 Wairau Road,
Auckland 10, New Zealand

Penguin Books Ltd, Registered Offices:
Harmondsworth, Middlesex, England

First published in 1995 by Viking Penguin,
a division of Penguin Books USA Inc.
This edition published by arrangement with Martin I. Green and Berkshire Studio

1 3 5 7 9 10 8 6 4 2

Copyright © Berkshire Studio Productions, Inc., 1995
All rights reserved

ISBN 0-670-86789-6
CIP data available

Printed in the United States of America

A BIO-GRAPHIC™ Produced by

BERKSHIRE
STUDIO
West Stockbridge, Massachusetts 01266

CREDITS & ACKNOWLEDGMENTS

Created, Designed & Produced by.................MARTIN I. GREEN
Illustrated & Designed by......................BILL SIENKIEWICZ
Original Script by..............................JEFF YOUNG
Adapted by.................ROSS FIRESTONE, MARTIN I. GREEN
& BILL SIENKIEWICZ
Edited by......................................ROSS FIRESTONE
Letterer & Associate Art Director..............BOBBI BONGARD
Research Director & Editorial Associate.........LELAND STEIN
Creative Consultant............................WILL EISNER
Creative Consultant & Editorial Associate.......JARED F. GREEN
Associate Creative Consultant..............MARY SIPP-GREEN
Production Associate.........................LEE EVERETT
Editorial & Administrative Associate..............EILEEN TAFT
Editorial Associate...........................CIA ELKIN
Image Research Director.......................BILL NITOPI
Project Consultant, Research Assistance
& Jimi Hendrix Quote Compilation......MICHAEL FAIRCHILD
Research Associate............................JOEL BRATTIN
Legal Advisor.................................ADRIA HILLMAN
Financial Advisor..........................LEO K. BARNES, CPA
Color Separation & Film.........................PREP, INC.

Our heartfelt gratitude to Alan Douglas for giving us the opportunity
to make this special project happen, and for his years of ongoing
encouragement, enthusiasm and support. Thank you, Alan.

Thanks also to the following for all the help they so magnanimously provided.

Maxine Martens and the staff of Are You Experienced?, Ltd. for making their resources
so readily available, and for all the other assistance they gave us.

Don Williams, Don Williams Music Group, Inc. and Bella Godiva Music, Inc.
for their unstinting cooperation.

Harry Shapiro, co-author of *Jimi Hendrix: Electric Gypsy*, for being so generous
with his time, knowledge and research. Your help was invaluable.

The late Bill Graham, whose interview with us was spirited,
combative and immensely inspiring.

Stella Shapiro for her wonderful stories and special insights into Jimi.

London Weekend Television for granting us permission to make use of
the materials in the Southbank documentary, *Jimi Hendrix*.

Caesar Glebbeek, co-author of *Jimi Hendrix: Electric Gypsy* and editor of
Univibes; Steve Roby, editor of *Straight Ahead*; and Ken Voss, editor of *Jimi*;
for giving us access to their Jimi Hendrix archives.

Noel Redding for the dinners, the stories and the insights.

Al Hendrix for being Jimi's father, and for keeping us on the right track.

Monika Dannemann for her cooperation,
and for making her personal photos of Jimi available to us.

Jim Goodkind for his endless efforts on our behalf.

Marc Jaffe for his wisdom, guidance and friendship.

Peter Gethers for being there at the beginning
and staying the course until the very end.

Roger Cooper, who was always there in every way.

Harvey Kahn for his enthusiasm and assistance.

George Pratt for his good taste and insightful observations.

Baron Wolman, Linda McCartney and David Pearcy
for so generously allowing us to use their original materials for inspiration.

Alan Selby, Mary Campbell and the crew at Electric Lady Studios
for opening their doors to us.

Peggy Gordon, Lucia Douglas, Anne Sipp, Lynne West, Leo Garel, Carol Kowalski, Gail Firestone, Annie Young, Richard Rubinstein, Gloria Henry, Martha Donovan, Henry and Helen Green, and Ben Schawinsky for their continuous support and encouragement.
Special thanks to Peter Mayer, Marvin Brown and Michael Fragnito of Penguin USA and to Denis Kitchen and the gang at Kitchen Sink Press.
Virginia Lohle of Starfile for her assistance and cooperation.
Dave Zalenski for his high standards and tireless efforts.
The wonderful staff at the Surrey Hotel for making life a lot easier.
And all those who helped along the way: Jay Cimbak; Denys Cowan; Jim Fitzgerald; Bob Gasster of Select Guitars, Norwalk, Connecticut; Bob Evans and the staff at Identicolor Services; Arthur Evans; Jay Reeg; Hayden Crilley; Rounder Records; Bing Broderick; Kevin Stein; Tom Yeates; Ron Theisen and Ben Valkhoff.

SOURCES FOR JIMI HENDRIX LYRICS & POEMS

All Jimi Hendrix compositions are copyrighted by Bella Godiva Music, Inc., c/o Don Williams Music Group, Inc., and are printed by permission of Bella Godiva Music, Inc., c/o Don Williams Music Group, Inc. and Are You Experienced?, Ltd. Jimi Hendrix's private writings are printed by permission of Are You Experienced?, Ltd.

Page 9. Jimi's private writings.
Page 14. panels 2-3. "Belly Button Window." ©1971.
panels 7-8, 10. "Voodoo Chile." ©1968.
Page 15. "Gypsy Eyes." ©1968.
Page 16. "Gypsy Eyes." ©1968.
Page 19. "Little Wing." ©1968.
Page 20. Jimi's private writings.
Page 22. "Castles Made of Sand." ©1968.
Page 23. "Voodoo Chile." ©1968.
Page 25. "Hear My Train A'Comin'." ©1970, 1971.
Page 27. "One Rainy Wish." ©1968.
Page 29. "Power to Love." (a.k.a. "Power of Soul.") ©1970, 1975.
Page 30. "Castles Made of Sand." ©1968.
Page 31. panels 1-4. "Angel." ©1971.
panels 6-8. "Voodoo Chile." ©1968.
Page 32. "Astro Man." ©1971.
Page 38. "Highway Chile." ©1970.
Page 41. "Manic Depression." ©1967.
Page 42. "Message of Love." ©1970, 1975.
Page 43. "Message of Love." ©1970, 1975.
Page 44. "Manic Depression." ©1967.
Page 48. "My Friend." ©1971.
Page 56. "Stone Free." ©1973.
Page 57. "Straight Ahead." ©1971.
Page 58. "Spanish Castle Magic." ©1968.
Page 62. panel 8. "Stone Free." ©1973.
Page 64. "May This Be Love." ©1967.
Page 65. "Purple Haze." ©1967.
Page 68. "Are You Experienced?" ©1967.
Page 76. panel 1. "Foxy Lady." ©1967.
panel 10. "The Wind Cries Mary." ©1967.
Page 78. "If 6 Was 9." ©1968.
Page 81. "One Rainy Wish." ©1968.
Page 82. "Little Wing." ©1968.
Page 92. "House Burning Down." ©1968.

Page 93. Jimi's private writings.
Page 101. "Have You Ever Been (To Electric Ladyland)?" ©1968.
Page 103. "Earth Blues." ©1971.
Page 104. top of panel 1. Jimi's private writings.
bottom of panel 1. "Hear My Train A'Comin'." ©1970, 1971.
Page 105. "The Burning of the Midnight Lamp." ©1967.
Page 107. Jimi's private writings.
Page 108. Jimi's private writings.
Page 109. "Room Full of Mirrors." ©1970, 1971.
Page 111. top of panel 1. Jimi's private writings.
bottom of panel 1. "Third Stone From The Sun." ©1967.
Page 113. Jimi's private writings.
Page 116. "I Don't Live Today." ©1967, 1975.
Page 117. panel 2. "Machine Gun." ©1970, 1973.
panel 11. "Look Over Yonder." ©1971.
Page 118. Jimi's private writings.
Page 120. panel 1. "1983...(A Merman I Should Turn to Be)." ©1968.
panel 2. "Straight Ahead." ©1971.
Page 122. panels 7-9. "Ezy Rider." ©1971.
panels 10-11. Jimi's private writings.
panels 14-16. "Voodoo Child (Slight Return)." ©1968.
Page 123. panel 1. "Freedom." ©1971.
panel 2. "Straight Ahead." ©1971.
panels 5-6. Jimi's private writings.
Page 124. Jimi's private writings.
Page 126. "Angel." ©1971.
Page 127. middle of page. "Angel." ©1971.
bottom of page. "Voodoo Child (Slight Return)." ©1968.
Page 128. Jimi's private writings.

OTHER SOURCES

Page 7. "'Scuse Me While I Kiss The Sky." By John Sinclair. ©1994 John Sinclair. All rights reserved.
Illustration based on a photograph by Linda McCartney. Used by permission.
Page 62. panel 7. "Hey Joe." By William M. Roberts. ©1962 Third Story Music, Inc. Printed by permission.

INTRODUCTION

"Every life is inexplicable," writes Paul Auster. "No matter how many facts are told, no matter how many details are given, the essential thing resists telling." Certainly, when the life that we speak of is one that found its most perfect articulation in music, in a language beyond mere language, that "essential thing" seems always to elude the grasp of the biographer's art. Such a life was the astounding supernova of rock composer and guitarist Jimi Hendrix, and such an essence is what the authors of this unprecedented graphic narrative have sought to capture.

While *VOODOO CHILD* is not so much outright biography as speculative fantasy — or rather, as the subtitle suggests, a dreamwork that provides words and images to what has already been canonized as pop culture legend — it has earned its poetic licenses through the careful research of the Hendrix archivists and biographers who contributed their time and energies in the interest of this project's authenticity. With its roots firmly embedded in the factual aspects of Hendrix's life, *VOODOO CHILD's* departures from conventional biography represent not only a collaboration of diverse literary and graphic talents, but also a unique fusion of artistic forms that both defines and exceeds the boundaries of its genre.

Employing the graphic narrative format that has emerged as an outgrowth of 20ᵀᴴ-century representational genres — ranging from Franz Masereel's block print novels, Lionel Feininger's expressionist Sunday strips and Will Eisner's pioneering works of sequential art, to name a few — the artwork of Bill Sienkiewicz reinvents the possibilities of the form, taking it to new heights of emotional intensity and aesthetic beauty. The nine hundred individual illustrations that comprise this book provide an almost cinematic scope and fluidity that allow the authors of the text to explore the spaces between the historic facts, those spaces where Hendrix's life was truly lived and from which the music emerged. As a result, *VOODOO CHILD's* unique integration of graphic and textual elements produces a constantly shifting mode of narrative that at every turn gestures beyond traditional structure toward the kind of sinewy musicality that made Hendrix's work so compelling both in his time and ours. This is the dimension that no biography, regardless of its individual merits, has been able to render until now. But *VOODOO CHILD* has done away with that limitation, and the fact that one cannot help but hear music coursing through the motion and colors of its images is the great achievement of this book, for the life of Hendrix is, after all, about the music more than anything else.

Listening again to Hendrix's recordings as I write this introduction, I'm put in mind of the immortal opening to Thomas Pynchon's *Gravity's Rainbow*: "A screaming comes across the sky. It has happened before, but there is nothing to compare it to now." While the reference here is to the fall of the German V-1 rocket, a slight shift from the war theater to the rock arena makes this metaphor seem just as appropriate for expressing the sheer power unleashed by a Hendrix guitar solo; the power not only to simultaneously destroy and reconstruct the notes as they were played, but also to refigure the experience of those who were listening. For members of my generation, now approaching our mid-to-late twenties, and accustomed from childhood to a blizzard of rock styles, including the *sturm und drang* of punk, industrial, and heavy metal, it is perhaps impossible to imagine what it might have been like to encounter Hendrix's music for the first time; to drop the needle on the initial track of *Are You Experienced* and feel the crunching opening chords of "Purple Haze" hit us square in the solar plexus. Or perhaps we do have some idea, for it is a testament to the enduring qualities of Hendrix's music that even in his absence, he has continued to have a palpable presence that shows no sign of diminishing. In fact, from the sonic assault of "Voodoo Chile" to the orgasmic shuffling funk-blues of "Crosstown Traffic," from the experimental electronic washes of "1983...(A Merman I Should Turn To Be)" to the tender instrumentation of ballads like "Angel" and "Castles Made of Sand," the imprint of Hendrix's virtuosity is still audible in nearly every genre of contemporary rock music. The ceaseless innovations that he brought both to the guitar and to rock composition overall may well account for the fact that, almost thirty years after *Are You Experienced* was first recorded, his music still sounds fresh and challenging to each successive generation of listeners and musicians, long after many of his contemporaries have been relegated to the fossil records of "classic rock." If there is any question as to why so many of the most popular and ambitious musicians of this decade place Hendrix foremost among their pantheon of heroes, the answer lies in the fact that he did not simply expand on an existing tradition, but actually defined an entirely new vocabulary for the electric guitar, and in doing so, laid down a blueprint with which all subsequent guitarists would have to contend. I think it hardly seems like an overstatement to say that after Hendrix, rock musicians had to make a choice: they could either approach the guitar as traditionalists, or they could accept the challenge to pursue the limitless possibilities that Hendrix's prodigious talent had made available.

That his life was so brief gives that much more reason to speculate what might have been: where his musical interests might have taken him and rock music itself. We have heard of the intended recording sessions he was to have with legendary trumpeter Miles Davis, and we can hear the inflections of jazz percolating through his last recordings. We can wonder if this might have been the direction he was beginning to pursue, or if it was only one more turn in the labyrinth of his musical explorations. But beyond the speculation that is invited by every great unfinished work — and surely Hendrix's life must be considered such a work — we know that the seismic upheaval he brought upon rock music is still producing aftershocks to this day. In its wake, what remains is a surprisingly extensive body of work, the legacy of his voracious musical appetites and ceaseless jam sessions with a host of musicians from all manner of musical backgrounds. We have his poetry and personal writings, many of which have been woven into the text of this book in the hope of capturing the true texture of both his public and private voices. We also have the remarkable recordings contained on the CD that accompanies this book. Like reading the lost manuscripts of a great author, these spontaneous and intimate sessions — captured on a simple reel-to-reel tape recorder while Hendrix was working out his new songs at home — allow us the rare opportunity to follow the progress of an imagination in the act of creation. Here we find the erasures, the marginalia, the chance accidents that would otherwise be no more than invisible traces within the finished product. Moreover, in the raw vitality of these tracks, we can hear exactly the kind of spirit of invention that *VOODOO CHILD* has managed to capture in its pages, a spirit that revealed itself in the vulnerability of the poetry, that articulated itself in the meticulous craftsmanship of the recordings and that unleashed itself in the incendiary dynamism of the live performances. Somewhere in the confluence of all of these elements is that essential thing that has for so long resisted telling; that thing that made Jimi Hendrix so legendary in his time, and the thing that, in finally being told, makes *VOODOO CHILD* a legend for our time.

—Jared F. Green

FOR JAMES MARSHALL HENDRIX

Up from the skies
over Seattle
like a Boeing jet
out of Mississippi,

guitar blazing fire
out of Elmore James
& Muddy Waters, Chuck Berry
& Little Richard,

taking stage after stage
back & forth across the country,
laying it down for the Queen
of Rock & Roll,

then it's Jimmy James & his Jammers
at the Cafe Wha?
in New York City,
Greenwich Village stylee,

guitar paratrooper
dropping from the skies over America
with the bomb
in his front pocket

& Miles Davis
on the phone, Gil Evans
listening
& taking notes,

Every guitar player
in England & America
tuned in to his frequencies
for everything they're worth —

Jimi Hendrix, baby,
blowing up the music
into something as vast
as the inside of his head,

fitting the music
around his pounding heart
& the explosions going off
inside his nerve endings,

the colors on the wall,
on his back & in-
side his cranium, the colors
of all colors,

colors of rhythm,
colors of blues,
colors of guitar string
& Marshall amplifiers

stacked up high
over his head,
colors of explosions
& bombs bursting in air,

Jimi changed the music
forever, in so
many different ways,
he changed the music

like it's never been changed
in all the years since, he took the colors
of everything in life
& put them right in the music

where they belong
& made it sing colors
without end, kissing the sky
again & again & again

—JOHN SINCLAIR

EEOOOWEEOOOWEEOOOV

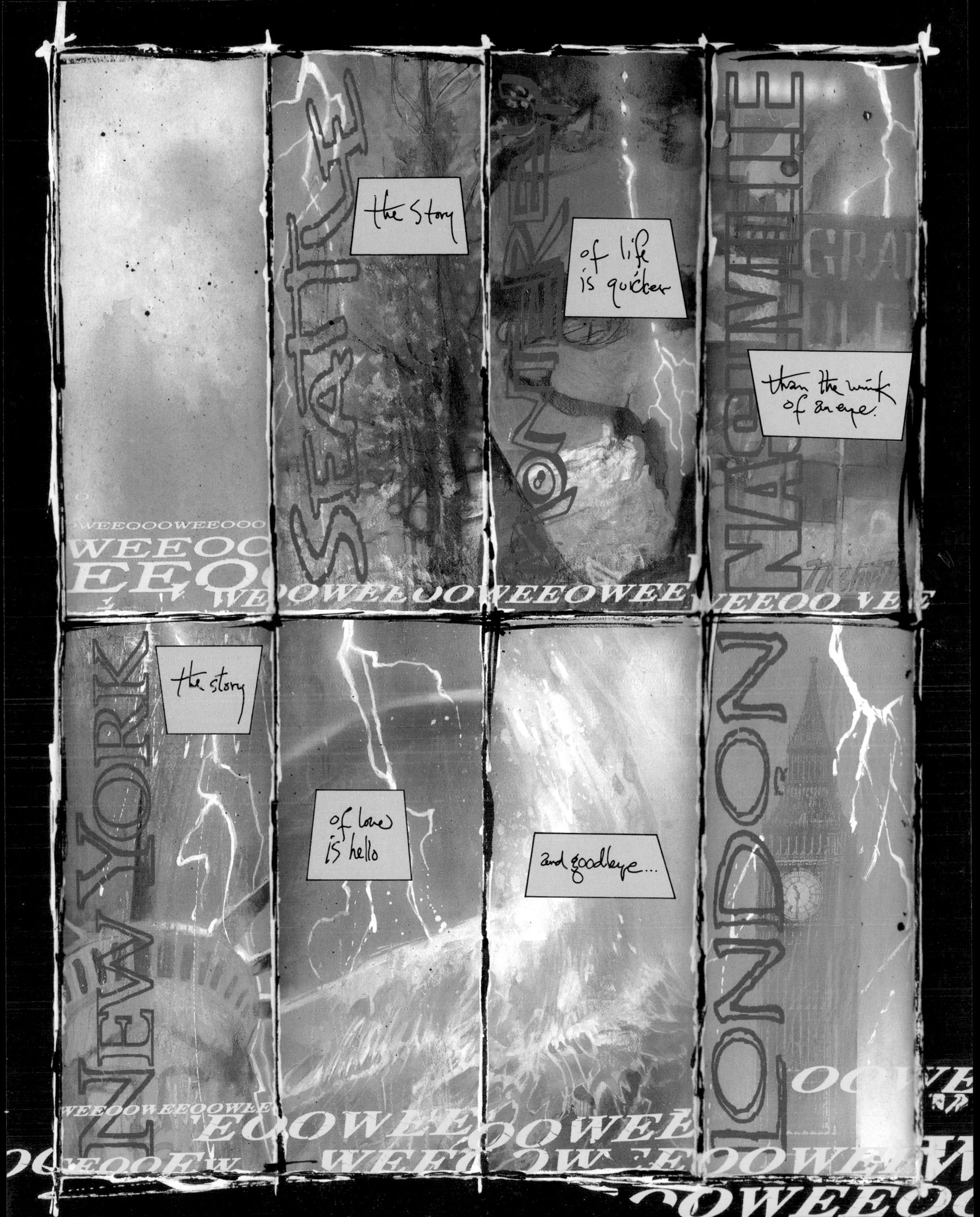
the Story
of life is quicker
than the wink of an eye.
the story
of love is hello
and goodbye...

OWEEOOOWEEOOO

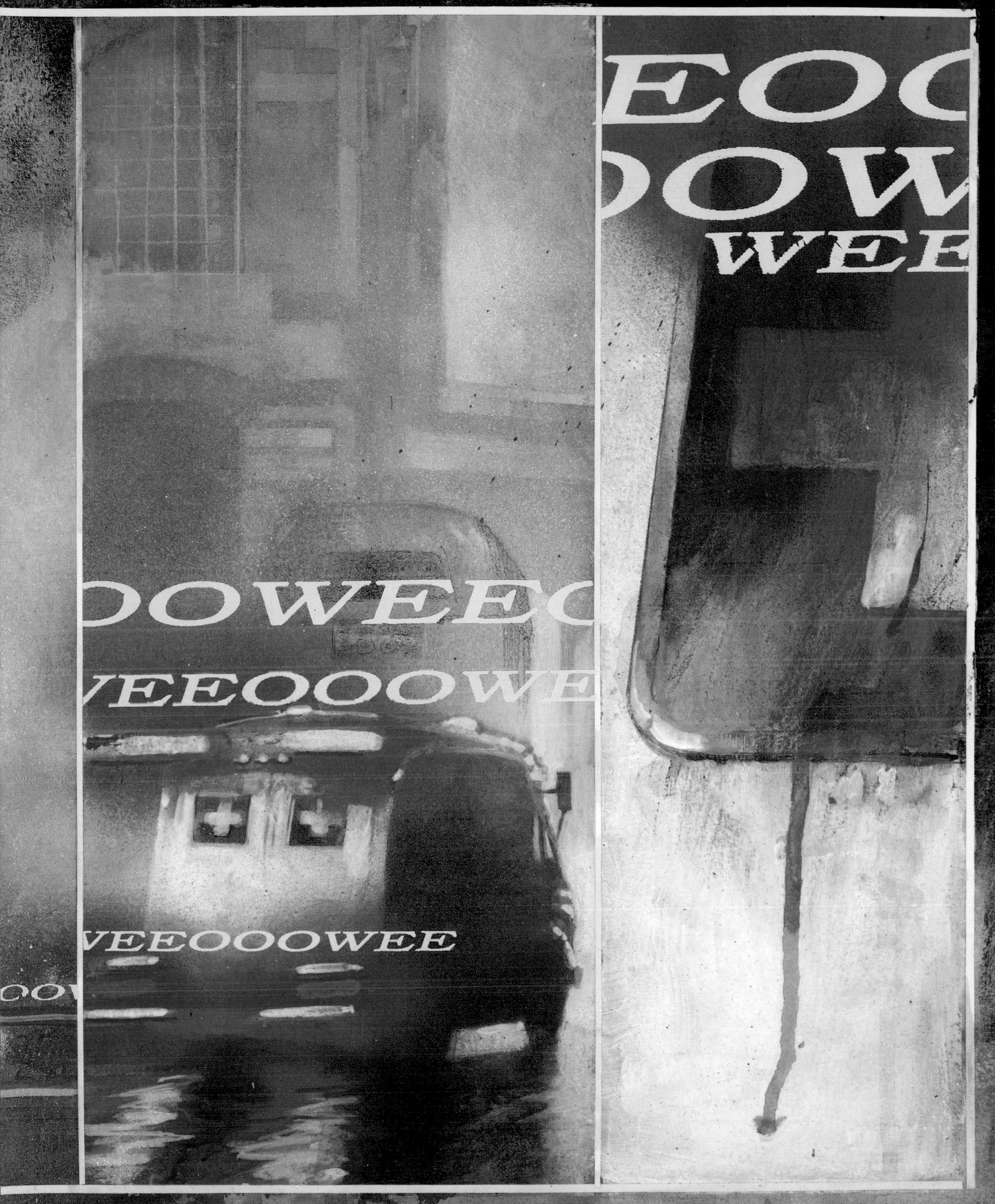
EOO
OOW
WEE
OOWEEO
VEEOOOWE
VEEOOOWEE
OOV

OOOOWE

WEE OOWEEOOWE OOWEEOOO

OOWEE CO

WEE OO

NOW?
SO SOON?
...LIKE THIS?

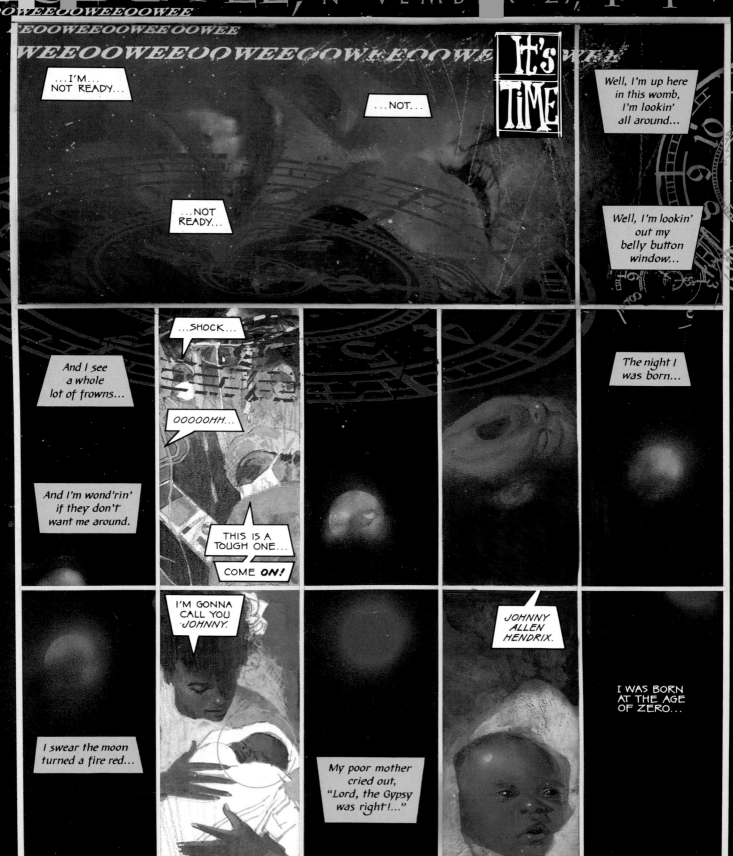

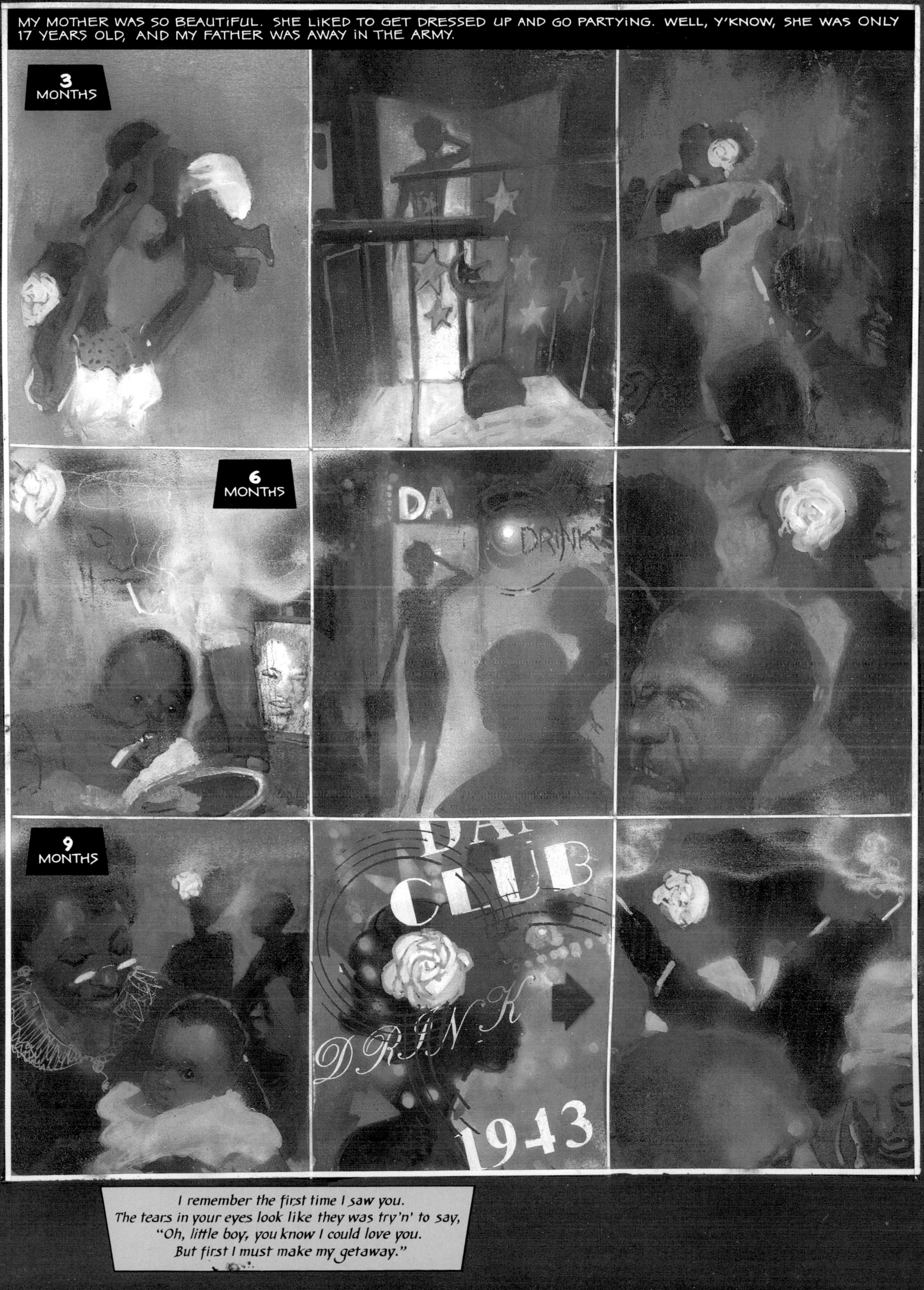

MY MOTHER WAS SO BEAUTIFUL. SHE LIKED TO GET DRESSED UP AND GO PARTYING. WELL, Y'KNOW, SHE WAS ONLY 17 YEARS OLD, AND MY FATHER WAS AWAY IN THE ARMY.

3 MONTHS

6 MONTHS

9 MONTHS

I remember the first time I saw you.
The tears in your eyes look like they was try'n' to say,
"Oh, little boy, you know I could love you.
But first I must make my getaway."

15

SHE WAS A GROOVY MOTHER...

...BUT SHE DIDN'T TAKE CARE OF HERSELF.

SOMETIMES SHE HAD TO GO TO THE HOSPITAL...

WEEOOWEEOO
WEEOOWE
EOOWEEOOWEEO
EOOWEEO

...AND SOMETIMES SHE WOULD JUST DISAPPEAR...

I WAS PASSED AROUND FROM ONE RELATIVE AND NEIGHBOR TO ANOTHER. I WAS LIKE A LITTLE GYPSY.

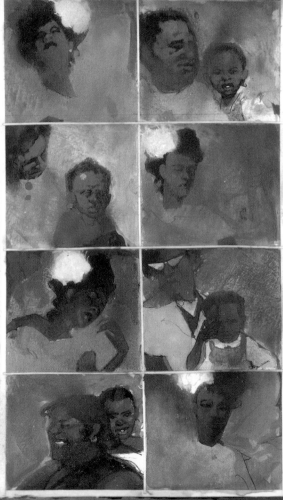

Way up in my tree I'm sitting by my fire,
Wond'rin' where in this world might you be.
And knowin' all the time you still are roamin' the countryside.
Do you still think about me?
Oh, my Gypsy...

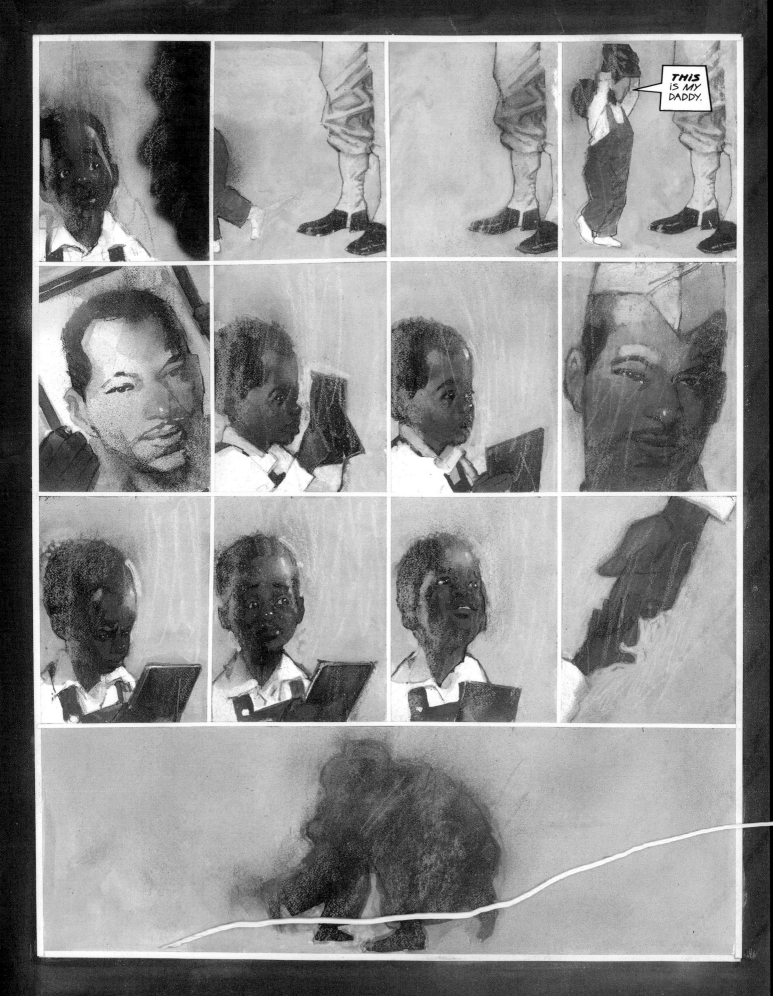

A FEW MONTHS LATER MY MOTHER CAME HOME AGAIN.

JOHNNY! OH, JOHNNY. MY SWEET JOHNNY... I'VE COME BACK TO YOU.

SOLDIER!

SOLDIER! FRONT AND CENTER! DOUBLE TIME!

JIMMY?... HMMM!

WELL THEN, ALRIGHT, JIMMY, LET'S HAVE A LOOK AT YOU...

LUCILLE, IT'S JIMMY NOW. JAMES MARSHALL HENDRIX.

When I'm sad she comes to me
With a thousand smiles she gives to me free.
"It's alright," she says.

"It's alright..."

FOR A WHILE WE WERE ALL REALLY HAPPY. THEY WENT OUT TOGETHER ALMOST EVERY NIGHT.

The best thing that happened to me since I was a little child —
I heard the cry of a guitar, and my heart went wild...

WHEN I WAS FIVE YEARS OLD MY BROTHER LEON WAS BORN.

MY MOTHER AND FATHER STARTED HAVING A LOT OF TROUBLE GETTING ALONG. SOMETIMES THEIR ARGUING SCARED ME SO MUCH I'D HIDE IN MY BED, TURN UP THE RADIO AND TRY TO DROWN IT OUT WITH THE BLUES...

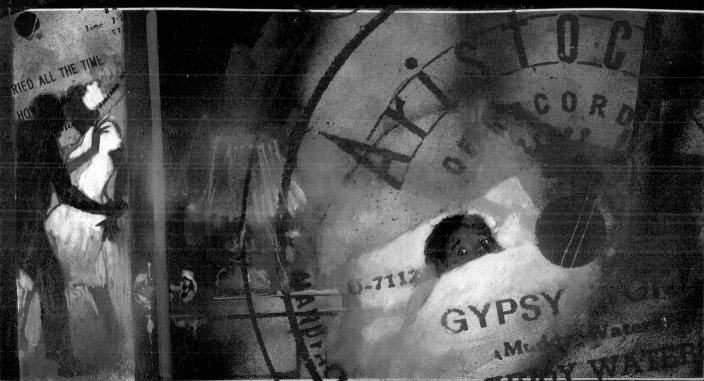

THEY USED TO BREAK UP ALL THE TIME, AND SOMETIMES I HAD TO GO TO CANADA TO STAY WITH MY GRANDMOTHER. SHE WAS A FULL-BLOODED CHEROKEE.

It's ALMOST time, JIMI...

GRANNY NORA WOULD MAKE PONCHOS FOR ME TO WEAR AS SHE'D SPIN OLD INDIAN TALES.

A little Indian brave,
Who before he was ten,
Played war games in the woods
With his Indian friends,

And he built a dream that
When he grew up,
He would be a fearless
Warrior Indian chief.

I LOVED GRANNY NORA VERY MUCH. SHE WAS A GREAT COMFORT TO ME, AND SO FAMILIAR. SO VERY FAMILIAR. SHE TAUGHT ME ALL KINDS OF THINGS... ESPECIALLY HOW YOU GOTTA LET YOUR MIND AND FANCY FLOW, FLOW, FLOW FREE...

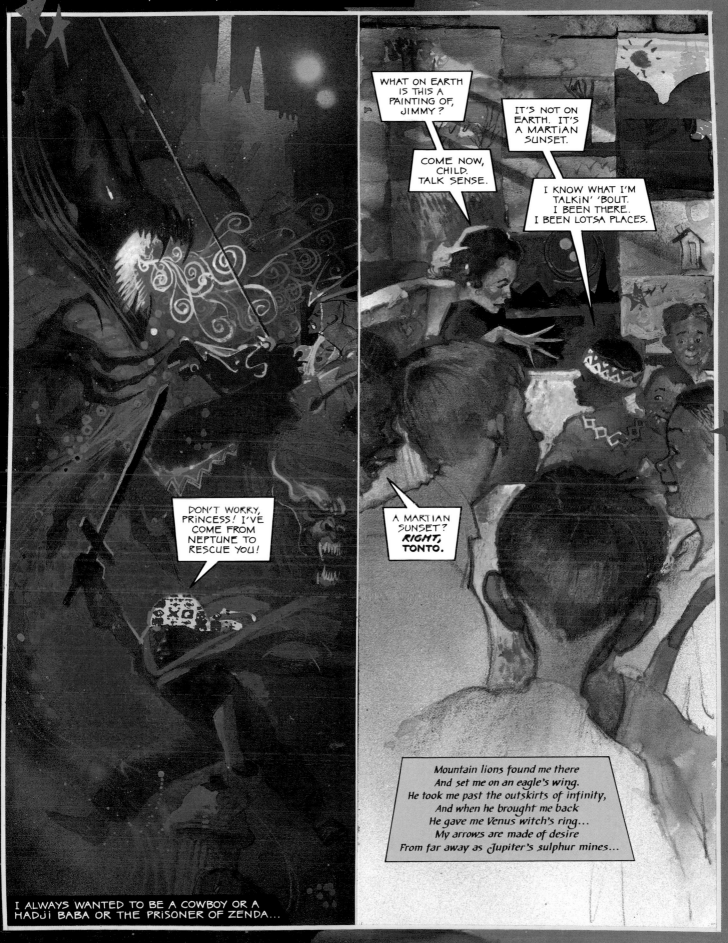

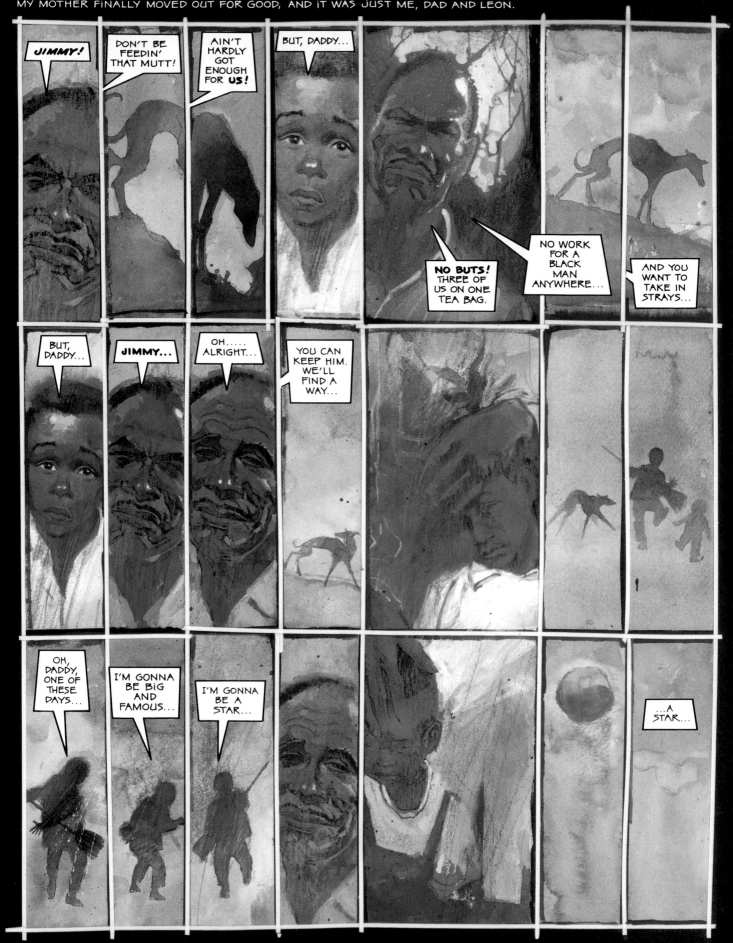

JIMMY, I'M SO PROUD OF YOU. I'M THE PROUDEST MAMA IN THE WHOLE WORLD.

I HAD THIS DREAM...

ZZZZZZZ MMMMMOM

ZZZZ...NO, MAMA... WHERE YOU...

W-WHERE YOU GOING?

WELL, I'M GONNA SEE YOU NOW...

I WON'T BE SEEING YOU MUCH ANYMORE, SO I'LL SEE YOU...

NO! DON'T GO! DON'T...

...And so castles made of sand Slip into the sea, Eventually.

30

A little boy inside a dream just the other day,
His mind fell out of his face,
And the wind blew it away.
A hand came out from Heaven
And pinned a badge on his chest,
And said, "Get out there, man,
And do your best."

YOUR HEART MAY BELONG TO MAMA BUT YOUR ASS BELONGS TO ME!

I FIGURED I'D HAVE TO GO INTO THE ARMY SOONER OR LATER, SO I VOLUNTEERED. I WANTED TO GET EVERYTHING OVER WITH BEFORE I TRIED TO GET INTO MUSIC AS A CAREER...

FORT CAMPBELL, KENTUCKY. NOVEMBER 1961

Dear Dad,
I made up my mind that whatever happens, I'm not quitting on my own... I'll try my very best to make this Airborne for the sake of our name.

OH, WHEN YOU FIRST JUMP, IT'S OUTASIGHT. SOME OF THEM CATS **NEVER** EVEN BEEN IN A PLANE BEFORE. SOME GUYS WERE THROWIN' UP IN A BIG BUCKET — A BIG GARBAGE CAN SITTIN' IN THE MIDDLE.

IT WAS GREAT. AND THE PLANE WAS GOIN' *RRROOOOOAARRR!!!* JUST ROARIN' AND SHAKIN' SO HARD YOU COULD SEE RIVETS JUMPIN'—

TALK ABOUT WHAT AM I DOIN' HERE? YOU'RE JUST THERE AT THE DOOR, AND ALL OF A SUDDEN, *FLOP! RUSH!* FOR A SPLIT SECOND A THOUGHT WENT THROUGH ME LIKE, "YOU'RE CRAZY!"

PHYSICALLY IT WAS A FALLING OVER BACKWARDS FEELING, LIKE IN YOUR DREAMS.

IT'S REAL PERSONAL, 'COS ONCE YOU GET OUT THERE, EVERYTHING'S SO QUIET.

ALL YOU HEAR IS THE BREEZE *SSSSHHHHHHH* LIKE THAT.

YOU'RE THERE ALL BY YOURSELF; YOU CAN TALK VERY LOW OR YOU CAN SCREAM, OR ANYTHING.

AND THEN YOU THINK ABOUT HOW CRAZY YOU ARE FOR DOING THIS, BUT I LOVED IT ANYWAY.

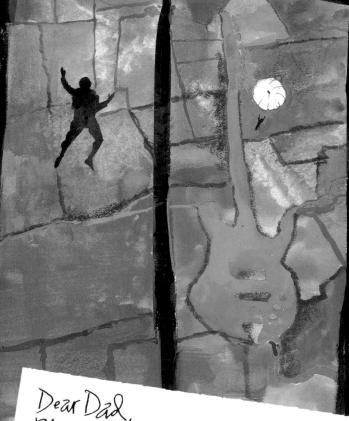

Dear Dad,
Please send my guitar as soon as you can — I really need it now...

OTHER THAN THE THRILL OF THE JUMP, HAVING MY GUITAR WAS THE ONLY THING THAT KEPT ME TOGETHER THEN. I PLAYED IT EVERY CHANCE I GOT — I DIDN'T CARE WHAT ANYONE ELSE THOUGHT, I JUST KEPT PLAYING!

MESS HALL

ENLISTED MEN'S LATRINE

YOU'VE MADE IT, MEN. I'M PROUD OF YOU, AS YOU SHOULD BE OF YOURSELVES. YOU CAN NOW WEAR THE BADGE OF PRIDE. YOU'VE EARNED IT.

CONGRATULATIONS.

YOU ARE NOW MEMBERS OF THE BEST UNIT OF THE U.S. ARMY: THE 101ST AIRBORNE.

AIRBORNE

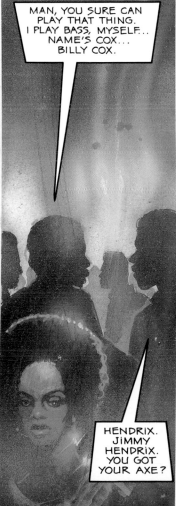

MAN, YOU SURE CAN PLAY THAT THING. I PLAY BASS, MYSELF... NAME'S COX... BILLY COX.

HENDRIX. JIMMY HENDRIX. YOU GOT YOUR AXE?

35

SO LONG, BILLY. I'LL BE WAITING FOR YOU IN NASHVILLE.

SEE YOU THERE, JIMMY.

His guitar slung across his back.
His dusty boots is his Cadillac.
Flamin' hair just a-blowin' in the wind.
Ain't seen a bed in so long it's a sin.

He left home when he was seventeen.
The rest of the world he went on to see.
And everybody knows, boss,
A rolling stone gathers no moss.
Now you'd probably call him a tramp.
But I know it goes a little deeper than that;

He's a Highway Chile.

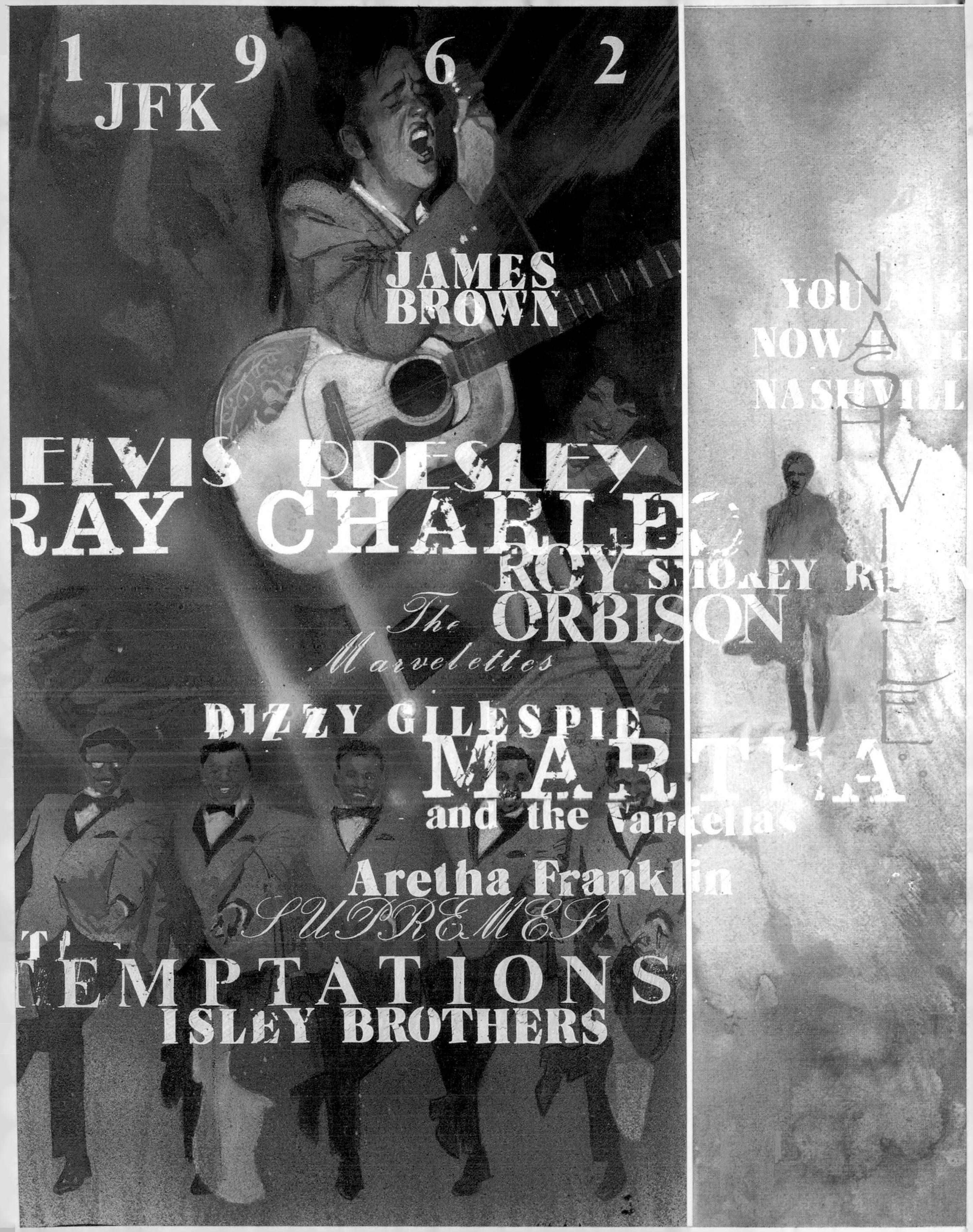
1 9 6 2
JFK
JAMES BROWN
ELVIS PRESLEY
RAY CHARLE
ROY ORBISON
The Marvelettes
DIZZY GILLESPI
MARTHA
and the Vandellas
Aretha Franklin
SUPREMES
TEMPTATIONS
ISLEY BROTHERS
NASHVILLE

IN NASHVILLE, EVERYONE PLAYED GUITAR. IT WAS LIKE ENTERING A COUNTRY WHERE WE ALL SPOKE THE SAME LANGUAGE.

BILLY ARRIVED, AND WE'D PLAY OUR AXES JUST ABOUT ANYPLACE...
...ANYTIME.

THE WOMEN WOULD HAVE TO WAIT.

WE DID SOME BACK-UP GIGS FOR SOME BETTER-KNOWN ACTS: NAPPY BROWN, CARLA THOMAS, IRONIN' BOARD SAM.

WE PLAYED A LOT OF BLUES.

I WAS WATCHING AND PLAYING AND WATCHING AND LEARNING ...ABOUT THE *SHOW* OF IT.

...SO I TRIED IT.

CROWDS SEEMED TO LIKE IT...

I WAS DOING IT FOR THEM, FOR THE *LOVE* OF IT...

AND BECAUSE I *HAD* TO DO IT.

HERE'S YOUR PAY FOR TONIGHT, GUYS.

...TWO DOLLARS?

IT WAS A SCUFFLE... I SLEPT WHERE I COULD, AND WHEN I NEEDED TO EAT I HAD TO STEAL IT. BUT I HAD THESE DREAMS THAT SOMETHING WAS GOING TO HAPPEN. I KEPT SEEING ONE-NINE-SIX-SIX IN MY DREAMS. I HAD VERY STRANGE FEELINGS THAT I WAS HERE FOR SOMETHING AND I WAS GOING TO GET A CHANCE TO BE HEARD... I GOT THE GUITAR TOGETHER BECAUSE THAT WAS ALL I HAD...

Manic Depression's touching my soul. I know what I want, But I just don't know how to go about gettin' it... Music, sweet music, I wish I could caress and, ah, kiss, kiss. Manic Depression's a frustrating mess.

IT WAS TIME TO SEE GRANNY NORA AGAIN...

41

I'M REALLY LEARNING TO PLAY IN NASHVILLE. YOU HAVE TO. PEOPLE THERE HEAR THE BLUES ALL THE TIME.
THEY SIT ON THEIR PORCHES ALL DAY PLAYIN' GUITAR...
I said find yourself first
And then your talent.
Work hard in your mind
For it to come alive.
I STARTED PLAYING WITH A LOT OF GROUPS ON THE CHITLIN' CIRCUIT...
THE MARVELETTES
CURTIS MAYFIELD
THE IMPRESSIONS
GORGEOUS GEORGE
ODELL
SAM COOKE
JACKIE WILSON
SLIM HARPO
THE SUPREMES
HANK BALLARD
YOU LISTEN AND LEARN, JIMMY. THAT'S VERY GOOD... BUT YOU MUST ALSO LISTEN TO THE SPIRITS. THEY SPEAK IN YOUR DREAMS. YOUR TIME WILL COME. BE PATIENT...WORK...
...AND LEARN TO BE **FREE.**
I'M TRYIN'.

IT WAS 1964. THE TIMES WERE CHANGING, BUT I WAS STILL HAVING TO PLAY THE SAME OLD STUFF...

BROTHERS, WE *GOT* TO HAVE A MEETING...

I AM LITTLE RICHARD. I AM THE KING OF ROCK AND RHYTHM, AND I'M THE ONLY ONE THAT'S GOING TO LOOK PRETTY ON STAGE!

GLYN AND JIMMY, WILL YOU PLEASE TURN IN THOSE SHIRTS, OR ELSE YOU WILL HAVE TO SUFFER THE CONSEQUENCES OF A FINE.

AND JIMMY, THAT GOES FOR YOUR HAIR, TOO. CUT IT.

I'M NOT CUTTIN' MY HAIR FOR *NOBODY.*

WELL, THEN, JIMMY... THAT WILL BE A FIVE DOLLAR *FINE...*

WHY DON'T YOU JUST TAKE IT OUT OF THE PAY YOU STILL OWE ME?

HMMMPH!

SLAM

THE FIRST GUITARIST I WAS AWARE OF WAS MUDDY WATERS. I HEARD ONE OF HIS RECORDS WHEN I WAS A LITTLE BOY AND IT SCARED ME TO DEATH, BECAUSE I HEARD ALL THOSE SOUNDS. WOW! WHAT WAS *THAT* ALL ABOUT? IT WAS GREAT!... GOING TO CHESS RECORDS, WHERE ALL THOSE GREAT BLUES GUYS RECORDED, WAS LIKE VISITING A SHRINE...

...AND WHEN THE MUSICIANS IN THE STUDIO LET ME PLAY FOR THEM, I FELT LIKE I'D BECOME PART OF IT...

I THOUGHT I WAS DOING GREAT... REALLY WAILIN'...
MUDDY DIDN'T SAY A WORD. HE JUST PICKED UP A GUITAR AND STARTED PLAYING...

AND THEN I REMEMBERED WHAT GRANNY NORA TOLD ME...

52

ON A GIG WITH CURTIS KNIGHT AND THE SQUIRES, MY GIRLFRIEND SPOTTED A COUPLE OF RECORD GUYS, SO I REALLY GOT INTO IT AND LET IT FLY...

YOU'LL BE HEARING FROM US...OH, UH, EXCUSE ME, MISS...

YOU'LL SIGN ANYTHING, 'LONG AS A MAN HANDS YOU A PEN AND A DOLLAR. ARE YOU *CRAZY!?*

SIGN *HERE*... AND *HERE*... GREAT, JIMMY! THANKS VERY MUCH.

BE COOL. I GOTTA START MAKIN' MY OWN RECORDS. DOLLAR DON'T MEAN NOTHIN' ANYWAY.

WHEN I WAS IN THE VILLAGE, DYLAN WAS STARVING DOWN THERE... I ONLY MET HIM ONCE, BACK AT THE KETTLE O' FISH ON MacDOUGAL STREET...WE JUST HUNG AROUND LAUGHING...

DYLAN REALLY TURNED ME ON AS A WAY TO GET MYSELF TOGETHER. A CAT LIKE THAT CAN DO IT TO YOU. I USED TO BE EMBARRASSED BY MY VOICE. DYLAN IS GOOD BECAUSE HE SINGS THE THINGS HE BELIEVES IN.

TRUE FEELINGS ARE REALLY THE ONLY QUALITIES WORTH LISTENING FOR IN A VOICE. I BEGAN TO BASE MY SINGING ON REAL FEELINGS AND TRUE THOUGHTS. I LEARNED THAT FROM LISTENING TO DYLAN.

Have you heard, baby,
What the wind's blowin' 'round?
Have you heard, baby?
A whole lot of people's coming right on down.
Communication, yeah, is comin' on strong.
It don't give a damn, baby,
If your hair is short or long.
I said get out of your grave.
Everybody is dancing in the street...

THE FIRST REAL GROUP I GOT TOGETHER ON MY OWN WAS BACK IN GREENWICH VILLAGE. I CHANGED MY NAME TO JIMMY JAMES AND CALLED THE GROUP THE BLUE FLAMES — NOT EXACTLY ORIGINAL, WAS IT?... MY BIG SLICE OF LUCK CAME WHEN MY FRIEND LINDA KEITH BROUGHT CHAS CHANDLER, THE BASS PLAYER WITH THE ANIMALS, DOWN TO WHERE WE WERE GIGGING, AND HE GAVE US AN EAR...

CHAS SAID HE WANTED TO BE MY MANAGER AND TAKE ME TO ENGLAND...HE SEEMED LIKE A PRETTY SINCERE GUY, AND I'D NEVER BEEN TO ENGLAND BEFORE... IT DIDN'T MATTER WHICH BIT OF THE WORLD I WAS IN, AS LONG AS I WAS LIVING AND PUTTING THINGS DOWN. PLUS, I COULD PLAY LOUDER OVER THERE, AND HE PROMISED TO INTRODUCE ME TO ERIC CLAPTON, THE FAIREST SOUL BROTHER IN THE LAND. BESIDES, WE WERE MAKING ABOUT THREE DOLLARS A NIGHT, AND WE WERE STARVING...OH, MAN! I DON'T THINK I COULD HAVE STOOD ANOTHER YEAR OF IT...I'M GLAD CHAS RESCUED ME...

I USED TO DREAM IN TECHNICOLOR THAT 1966 WAS THE YEAR SOMETHING WOULD HAPPEN TO ME... IT CAME TRUE. 1966 WAS MY YEAR — *IN TECHNICOLOR!*

CHAS SAID HE HAD A PLAN.
WE WERE GOIN' FOR BROKE.
IF IT WORKED I'D BE A BIG
STAR — FAST. IF NOT, WE'D
BOTH JUST BE BROKE.

Dear Dad,
I'm in England, Dad. I met some people
and they're going to make me a big star.
We changed my name to J-I-M-I.

THE IDEA WAS FOR ME TO PLAY AROUND AS MUCH AS
POSSIBLE AND GET HEARD BY THE "RIGHT" PEOPLE — THE
GUYS WHO LET THE REST OF THE WORLD KNOW WHAT'S
HAPPENIN'. THAT WAY WE COULD BE "DISCOVERED,"
SORT OF MAKE IT UP FROM THE "UNDERGROUND." CHAS
ARRANGED FOR ME TO START JAMMING RIGHT AWAY
AROUND THE VARIOUS CLUBS — BLAISES, LES COUSINS,
POLYTECHNIC OF CENTRAL LONDON AND SCOTCH OF
SAINT JAMES. HE KNEW JUST ABOUT EVERYBODY —
JEFF BECK, ERIC CLAPTON, PETE TOWNSHEND, PAUL
McCARTNEY, JOHN LENNON, MICK JAGGER, BRIAN
JONES — *EVERYBODY!*... THEY ALL SHOWED UP TO
CHECK ME OUT...

WE REALLY WEREN'T SURE WHAT SOUND WE WERE LOOKING FOR OR EVEN HOW MANY PIECES. I JUST KNEW I WANTED THE SMALLEST GROUP POSSIBLE WITH THE HEAVIEST IMPACT...

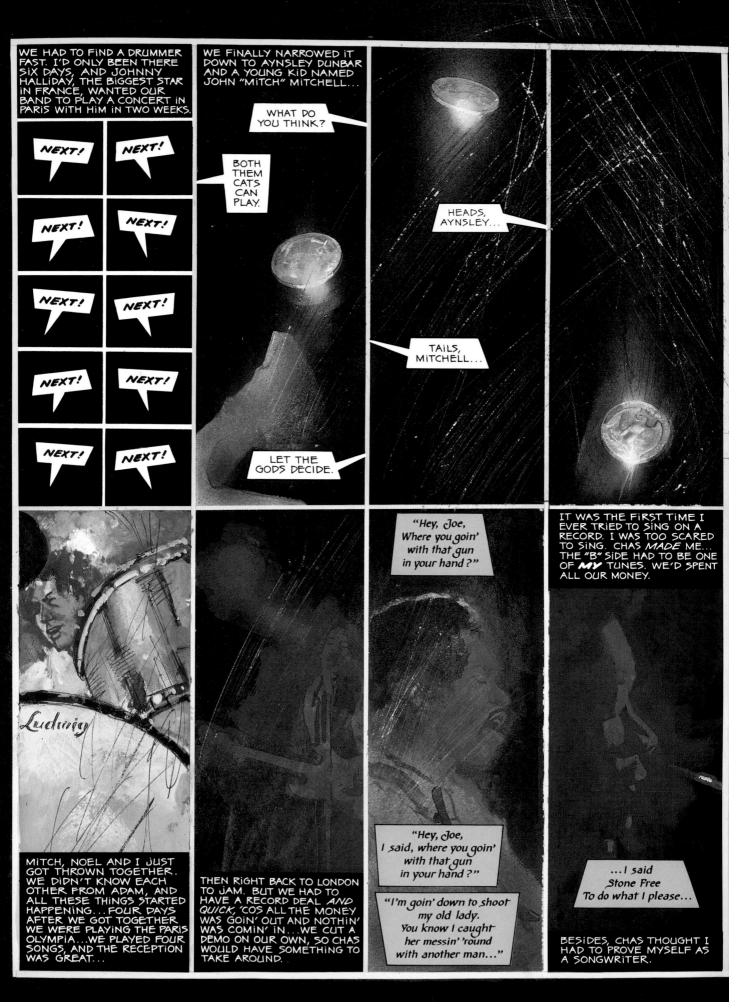

WE HAD TO FIND A DRUMMER FAST. I'D ONLY BEEN THERE SIX DAYS, AND JOHNNY HALLIDAY, THE BIGGEST STAR IN FRANCE, WANTED OUR BAND TO PLAY A CONCERT IN PARIS WITH HIM IN TWO WEEKS.

NEXT! NEXT!
NEXT! NEXT!
NEXT! NEXT!
NEXT! NEXT!
NEXT! NEXT!

WE FINALLY NARROWED IT DOWN TO AYNSLEY DUNBAR AND A YOUNG KID NAMED JOHN "MITCH" MITCHELL...

WHAT DO YOU THINK?

BOTH THEM CATS CAN PLAY.

LET THE GODS DECIDE.

HEADS, AYNSLEY...

TAILS, MITCHELL...

IT WAS THE FIRST TIME I EVER TRIED TO SING ON A RECORD. I WAS TOO SCARED TO SING. CHAS *MADE* ME... THE "B" SIDE HAD TO BE ONE OF *MY* TUNES. WE'D SPENT ALL OUR MONEY.

MITCH, NOEL AND I JUST GOT THROWN TOGETHER. WE DIDN'T KNOW EACH OTHER FROM ADAM, AND ALL THESE THINGS STARTED HAPPENING... FOUR DAYS AFTER WE GOT TOGETHER WE WERE PLAYING THE PARIS OLYMPIA... WE PLAYED FOUR SONGS, AND THE RECEPTION WAS GREAT...

THEN RIGHT BACK TO LONDON TO JAM. BUT WE HAD TO HAVE A RECORD DEAL *AND QUICK,* 'COS ALL THE MONEY WAS GOIN' OUT AND NOTHIN' WAS COMIN' IN... WE CUT A DEMO ON OUR OWN, SO CHAS WOULD HAVE SOMETHING TO TAKE AROUND.

"Hey, Joe, Where you goin' with that gun in your hand?"

"Hey, Joe, I said, where you goin' with that gun in your hand?"

"I'm goin' down to shoot my old lady. You know I caught her messin' 'round with another man..."

...I said Stone Free To do what I please...

BESIDES, CHAS THOUGHT I HAD TO PROVE MYSELF AS A SONGWRITER.

IT WAS CHAS' IDEA TO CALL THE GROUP *THE JIMI HENDRIX EXPERIENCE*...WE SET OUT TO BE A TRIP...THAT'S THE REASON WE WERE LIKE THAT. WE PLAYED *VERY, VERY* LOUD. WE WANTED TO CREATE A CERTAIN EFFECT, TO MAKE IT ALL AS PHYSICAL AS POSSIBLE. WE *REALLY* WANTED TO FREAK THEM OUT...

I DIDN'T MEAN TO BREAK IT...IF WE SMASH SOMETHING UP, IT'S BECAUSE THAT INSTRUMENT, WHICH IS SOMETHING YOU DEARLY LOVE, JUST ISN'T WORKING. IT'S NOT RESPONDING, AND SO YOU WANT TO KILL IT...I JUST LOST MY TEMPER AND SMASHED THE DAMN THING TO PIECES. THE CROWD WENT MAD...YOU'D HAVE THOUGHT I FOUND THE LOST CHORD OR SOMETHING...

THEY SAID ALL THOSE HEAD-LINES WERE JUST SHOW BIZ. THAT THE FREAKIER MY IMAGE, THE BETTER... THAT IT WOULD HELP GET THE "UNDERGROUND" ON MY SIDE... *YEAH, RIGHT!* THEY'D HAVE LOVED IT IF I LOOKED LIKE A CANNIBAL...

I TRIED NOT TO LET IT GET TO ME...

WE FINALLY GOT A RECORD DEAL AFTER BEING TURNED DOWN ALL OVER THE PLACE. BUT WITHOUT AIRPLAY, WE COULDN'T GO ANYWHERE.

AND IF WE DIDN'T HAVE A HIT WITH "HEY JOE," THEN NO BAND. THERE WAS NO MONEY LEFT, SO CHAS HAD TO HOCK HIS GUITARS TO KEEP US GOING. CHAS WAS SURE, BUT ME?... I JUST WISHED I COULD SING NICE...I WAS JUST FEELING THE WORDS OUT.

Waterfall,
Nothing can harm me at all.
My worries seem so very small
With my waterfall...
So let them laugh, laugh at me.
So just as long as I have you
To see me through,
I have nothing to lose,
'Long as I have you...

SO WE DID ANOTHER SERIES OF GIGS ANYWHERE WE COULD TO PAY THE RENT AND PROMOTE THE RECORD. WHEN WE STARTED, "HEY JOE" WAS ON THE CHARTS AT #48

MANCHESTER

LONDON

CAMBRIDGE

BERKSHIRE

OLDHAM

...AND ROSE TO #4. *WE HAD A HIT RECORD!* BUT THERE WAS STILL A LOT OF WORK TO DO.

HOTEL

WE CONTINUED TO TOUR...THIS TIME EUROPE...WE JUST KEPT MOVING — ONE TOWN, ONE COUNTRY AFTER ANOTHER. THEN BACK TO LONDON, WHERE WE WERE MET BY MORE FANS — *CROWDS OF 'EM!!* SOME EVEN CAMPED OUT IN FRONT OF OUR HOTEL...IT WAS GETTIN' PRETTY WILD... LOTS OF WONDERFUL THINGS WERE HAPPENING, INCLUDING KATHY ETCHINGHAM, A BEAUTIFUL ENGLISH GIRL WHO BECAME ONE OF THE MOST IMPORTANT WOMEN IN MY LIFE.

I WANTED TO CREATE NEW SOUNDS TO TRY TO TRANSMIT MY DREAMS TO THE AUDIENCE. AND WHEN BRIAN JONES AND I CRUISED AROUND IN HIS ROLLS, LISTENING TO THE ROLLING STONES' "RUBY TUESDAY," I *HAD* TO KNOW HOW THEY GOT IT TO SOUND THAT WAY...

MUSIC MUST ALWAYS CONTINUE TO EXPAND FURTHER OUT — FURTHER AWAY. "PURPLE HAZE" WAS ONE STEP ON THE WAY TO GETTING OUR *OWN* PERSONAL SOUND...

ME AND KEITH JUST WORKED AND WORKED ON IT, ADDING COLOR HERE AND THERE IN THE STUDIO. WE ADJUSTED THE MIX BETWEEN LEAD AND BACKGROUND VOCALS, AND ADDED A FEW EXOTIC INSTRUMENTS.

IT'S BEAUTIFUL!

Purple Haze all in my brain.
Lately things just don't seem the same.
Acting funny, but I don't know why.
'Scuse me while I kiss the sky.

Purple Haze all around.
Don't know if I'm comin' up or down.
Am I happy or in misery?
Whatever it is, that girl put a spell on me!...

Purple Haze all in my eyes.
Don't know if it's day or night.
You got me blowin', blowin' my mind.
Is it tomorrow or just the end of time?

65

I REALLY LEARNED A LOT ABOUT BRITISH AUDIENCES ON THAT TOUR BECAUSE EVERY NIGHT WE HAD TWO MORE TO MEET. THOSE THAT CAME TO HEAR ENGELBERT SING "RELEASE ME" MAY NOT HAVE DUG ME, BUT WE REFUSED TO CHANGE OUR ACT.

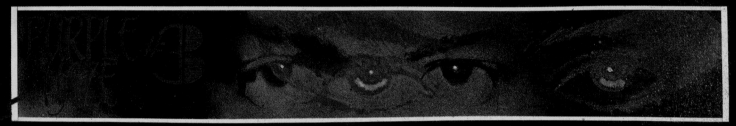

WHEN I WAS MOVING OUT THERE, I WAS JUST SQUEEZING THAT LITTLE BIT MORE OUT OF MY GUITAR...SOMETIMES I JUMPED UP ON THE GUITAR, SOMETIMES I WOULD GRIND THE STRINGS UP AGAINST THE FRETS. *THE MORE IT GRINDS, THE MORE IT WHINES*...IT WAS JUST THE WAY I PLAYED.

WE CUT "HEY JOE," AND THEN WE CUT "PURPLE HAZE," AND WE *MADE IT*, MAN! YOU KNOW, BECAUSE WE HAD OUR OWN THING AND IT REALLY WAS OUR OWN THING AND NOBODY ELSE'S AND WE PLAYED IT LIKE WE WERE FEELING...

I WANTED OUR FIRST ALBUM TO SHOW HOW WE PLAYED IN PERSON. I DIDN'T NECESSARILY WANT IT TO BE PERFECT... WHEN IT ALL COMES DOWN TO IT, ALBUMS ARE NOTHING BUT PERSONAL DIARIES. WHEN YOU HEAR SOMEBODY MAKING MUSIC, THEY ARE BARING A NAKED PART OF THEIR SOUL TO YOU... THE SONGS JUST CAME. IT WAS NERVE-RACKING BECAUSE I'D START WORKING ON A SONG IN THE STUDIO AND GET INSPIRATION WHILE WE WERE RECORDING. *ARE YOU EXPERIENCED* WAS ONE OF THE MOST DIRECT ALBUMS WE DID...WHAT IT WAS SAYING WAS, "LET US GET THROUGH THE WALL, MAN, WE WANT YOU TO DIG IT."

IT WAS A MIXTURE OF ROCK, BLUES AND JAZZ. AND IT HAD A FEW FREAK-OUT TUNES. A MUSIC THAT WAS JUST COMING. A MUSIC OF THE FUTURE. IT WAS A COLLECTION OF FREE FEELING AND IMAGINATION. IMAGINATION IS VERY IMPORTANT. MAYBE SOME OF THE STUFF WAS FAR AHEAD. I DON'T KNOW. I WAS VERY HAPPY WITH IT.

THE ALBUM WAS A BIG HIT AND BROUGHT US A WHOLE LOT OF ATTENTION...ENGLAND WAS OUT OF SIGHT, MAN...THEY TOOK US IN LIKE LOST BABIES...

WE WERE SOME OF THE LUCKIEST CATS ALIVE. WE WERE PLAYING JUST WHAT WE WANTED TO PLAY — WHAT GAVE US PLEASURE...AND PEOPLE SEEMED TO LIKE THAT...SOMETIMES THE AUDIENCE SAID "HOORAY" SO LOUD, IT SCARED ME OUT OF MY MIND. I WANTED TO SAY, "NOT SO LOUD." BUT I LIKED IT...IT MADE ME FEEL LIKE CRYING...

If you can just get your mind together,
Then come on across to me.
We'll hold hands,
And then we'll watch the sun rise
From the bottom of the sea...

IT HAD NEVER HAPPENED BEFORE! BY THE END OF THE THREE DAYS, OVER 90,000 KIDS SHOWED UP TO ROCK 'N' ROLL TO THE WHO, JANIS JOPLIN, THE GRATEFUL DEAD, OTIS REDDING, BUFFALO SPRINGFIELD, RAVI SHANKAR, THE MAMAS AND THE PAPAS, AND A TON OF OTHERS...NO ONE HAD EVER SEEN ANYTHING LIKE IT!!

ACTUALLY, I WAS SCARED TO GO OUT THERE AND PLAY IN FRONT OF ALL THOSE PEOPLE...YOU REALLY WANT TO TURN THOSE PEOPLE ON. IT'S A VERY DEEP CONCERN...YOU GET VERY INTENSE...

A VERY GOOD FRIEND, A FELLOW COUNTRYMAN OF YOURS, A BRILLIANT PERFORMER, THE MOST EXCITING STAR I'VE EVER HEARD...

...THE JIMI HENDRIX EXPERIENCE!

BUT ONCE YOU HIT THE FIRST NOTE, OR ONCE THE FIRST THING GOES DOWN, THEN IT'S ALL RIGHT. LET'S GET TO THOSE PEOPLE'S BUTTS! THAT'S WHAT I WANTED...

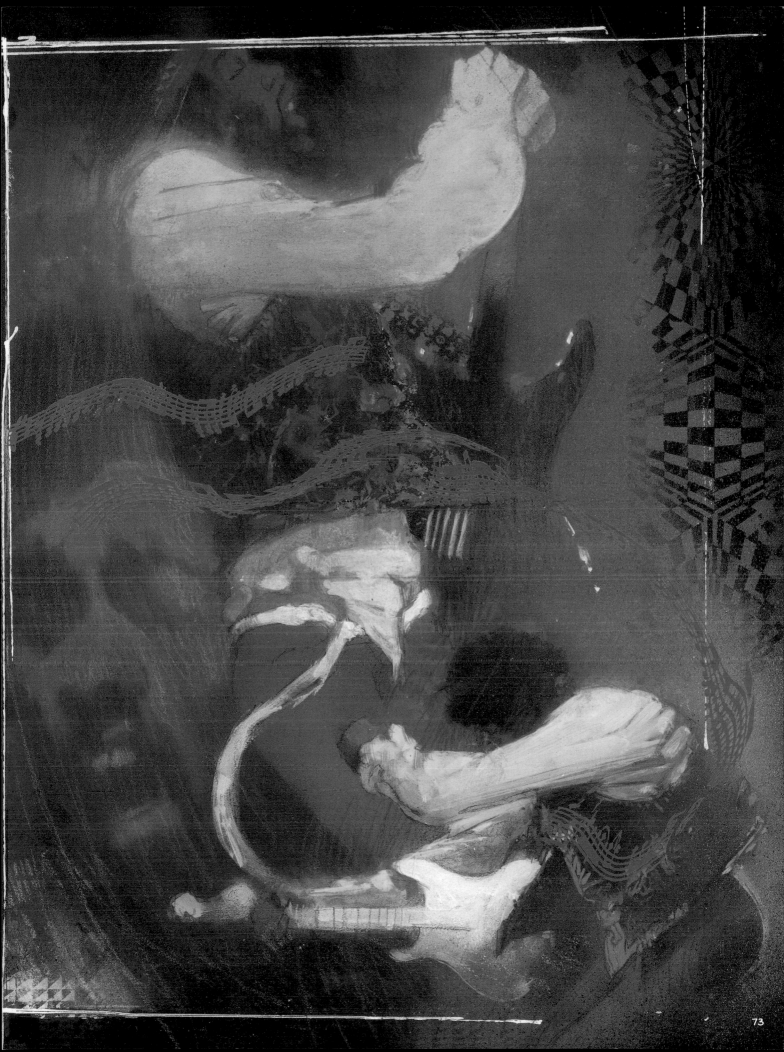

...AS LONG AS YOU WANT TO BELIEVE THE WORLD IS A STAGE, THEN APPOINT ME YOUR ELECTRIC STAGEHAND...AND I SHALL PRODUCE UPON YOU AN OVERWHELMING HURRICANE... STRAIGHT FROM YOUR OWN SCRIPT...

YOU KILLED THEM, MAN.
YOU *KILLED* THEM.

HENDRIX GRADUATES
FROM RUMOR TO LEGEND

You know you a cute little heartbreaker.
Yeah!
And you know you a sweet little love maker.
I wanna take you home, yeah.
I won't do you no harm, no.
You've got to be all mine, all mine.
Ooh, Foxy Lady!

HER NAME WAS DEVON WILSON. I MET HER AT THE WHISKEY AU GO GO. IT WAS SUMMER...

I SAW HER FROM ACROSS THE ROOM. OUR EYES MET. SHE SMILED...

WE NODDED TO EACH OTHER.

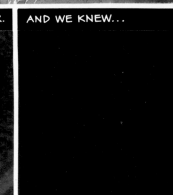

AND WE KNEW...

THAT WE'D ALWAYS BE TOGETHER...

JUST LIKE IN THE MOVIES...

HOUDINI USED TO LIVE IN MY HOUSE, JIMI. BUT **YOU** BETTER NOT EVEN THINK OF ESCAPIN'.

HEY, I'M AS HAPPY AS A STRAWBERRY...

After all the jacks are in their boxes,
And the clowns have all gone to bed,
You can hear happiness staggering on down the street,
Footprints dressed in red...

THE MONKEES WERE A PLASTIC BAND MADE UP FOR TELEVISION — STRICTLY FOR THE TEENYBOPPERS. THE KIDS WHO DUG THEM WOULDN'T HAVE THE SLIGHTEST IDEA WHERE I WAS COMING FROM.

I WAS GETTING KINDA SCARED. LIKE SOON I'D BE GOING INTO ANOTHER BAG WITH A NEW SOUND, A NEW RECORD, A NEW EXPERIENCE. WE WERE GOING TO GO EXACTLY THE WAY WE FELT. I DIDN'T KNOW WHICH WAY THAT'D BE. NOTHING WAS GOING TO BE INTENTIONAL. IT WOULD JUST HAPPEN.

...IN DEFERENCE TO THE DAUGHTERS OF THE AMERICAN REVOLUTION, WHO SEEM TO BE OUTRAGED BY THE JIMI HENDRIX EXPERIENCE, AND WHAT THEY FEEL TO BE VULGAR AND EROTIC WHEN THEY BROUGHT THEIR CHILDREN TO SEE THE MONKEES, THE JIMI HENDRIX EXPERIENCE WILL BE LEAVING THE TOUR EFFECTIVE IMMEDIATELY.

WE WEREN'T GOING TO TRY TO KEEP UP WITH THE TRENDS, BECAUSE WE HAD A CHANCE TO BE OUR OWN TREND.

IT WAS JUST THE WRONG AUDIENCE. I THINK THEY REPLACED ME WITH MICKEY MOUSE. THAT STUFF ABOUT THE D.A.R. WAS JUST A SHUCK, JUST ANOTHER WAY TO BUILD ME UP AS THE "WILD MAN." I WAS GETTING REAL WORN OUT BY THAT KIND OF SHIT.

IN *AXIS* THERE WERE MANY MORE GENTLE THINGS, MORE THINGS FOR PEOPLE TO THINK ABOUT IF THEY WANTED TO... THE EARTH TURNS ON ITS AXIS AND CHANGES THE FACE OF THE WORLD... IT'S THE SAME WITH LOVE. IT CAN TURN YOUR WHOLE WORLD UPSIDE DOWN... IT'S THAT POWERFUL, THAT BOLD...PEOPLE KILL THEMSELVES FOR LOVE, BUT WHEN YOU HAVE IT FOR SOMEBODY OR SOMETHING, AN IDEA, MAYBE, IT CAN BEAT ANGER AND TIME AND MOVE THE SEA AND MOUNTAINS...THAT'S THE WAY IT FEELS...I GUESS THAT'S WHAT I WAS TRYING TO SAY...

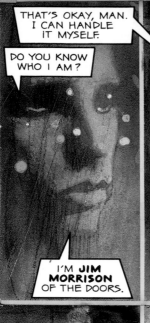

HEY, JIMI! JIMI! LET ME COME UP AND SING, MAN, AND WE'LL DO THIS SHIT TOGETHER...

THAT'S OKAY, MAN. I CAN HANDLE IT MYSELF.

DO YOU KNOW WHO I AM?

I'M **JIM MORRISON** OF THE DOORS.

YEAH, I KNOW WHO YOU ARE... AND I'M JIMI HENDRIX.

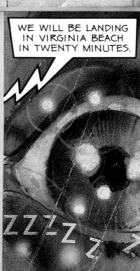

INSTRUMENTALIST OF THE WORLD - JIMI HENDRIX -

ZZZZZZZZ

ZZZZZ Z Z

WE WILL BE LANDING IN VIRGINIA BEACH IN TWENTY MINUTES.

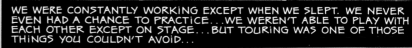

WE WERE CONSTANTLY WORKING EXCEPT WHEN WE SLEPT. WE NEVER EVEN HAD A CHANCE TO PRACTICE...WE WEREN'T ABLE TO PLAY WITH EACH OTHER EXCEPT ON STAGE...BUT TOURING WAS ONE OF THOSE THINGS YOU COULDN'T AVOID...

APRIL 4, 1968

...THIS NEWS FLASH...

MARTIN LUTHER KING'S BEEN SHOT.

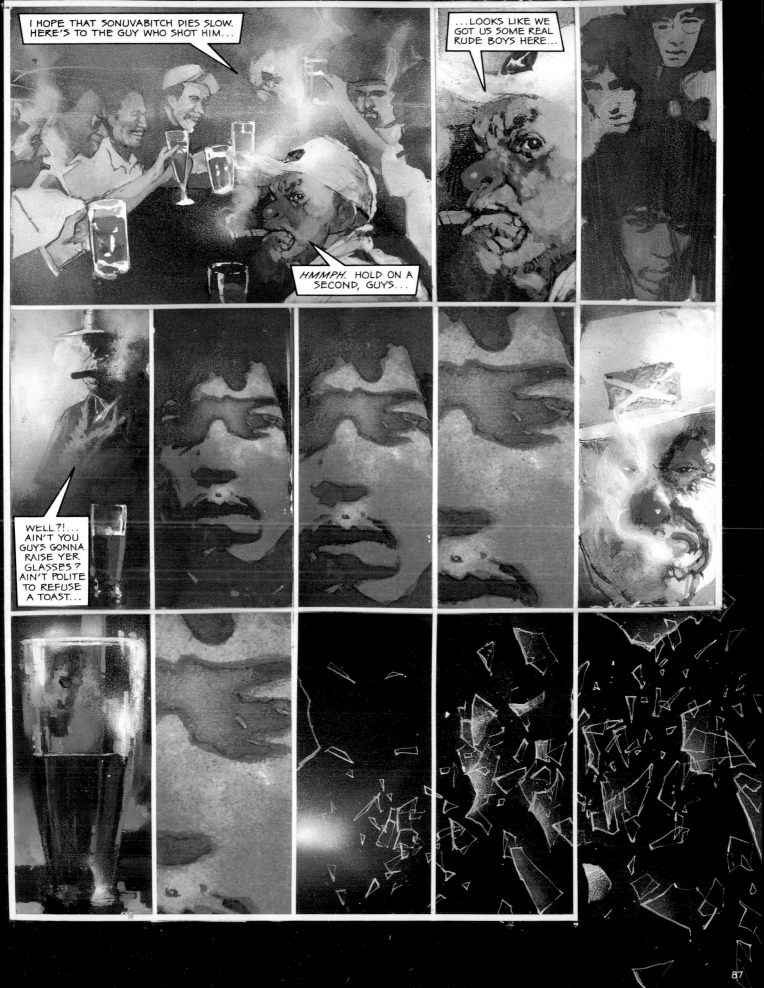

DR. KING'S MURDER SET OFF RIOTS, LOOTING AND FIRES EVERYWHERE...WE WERE BACK IN NEW YORK AND HAD TO DO A CONCERT THAT NIGHT IN NEWARK...EVERYONE WAS REALLY UPTIGHT...SCARED TO DEATH ABOUT WHAT MIGHT HAPPEN NEXT. WE TRIED TO CANCEL, BUT THE POLICE SAID IF WE DIDN'T SHOW, IT WOULD GET TOTALLY OUT OF HAND AND THEY WOULDN'T BE ABLE TO CONTROL THE CROWD AT THE ARENA...SO WE WENT...

OWEEOOO

OWEEO

WEEO
OWEEOO

OWEEOO

OWEEOO

WEEOOOW

WEEOOOW

NEWARK'S GOING TO MAKE NEW YORK LOOK LIKE A PICNIC!...

JIMI SITS UP FRONT WITH ME OR I DON'T GO...

LINCOLN TUNNEL to NEW JERSEY

OWEEO
OWEEOOOWEEOO

WEEO
OOWEEOOOWE

THIS IS THE PLACE.

SYMPHONY HALL

MAN, IT SURE FEELS WEIRD...

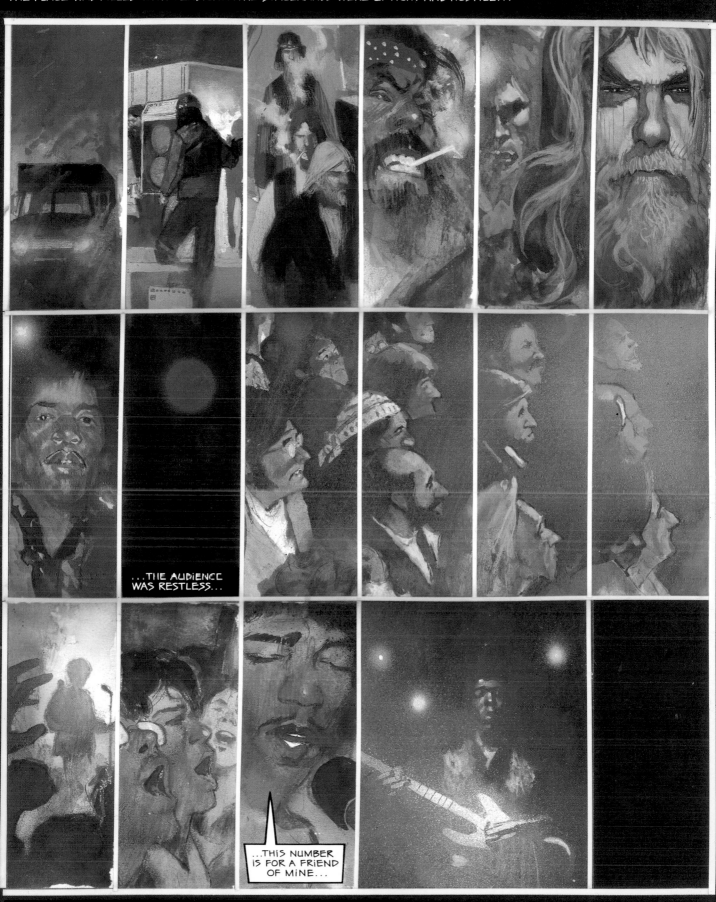

"I have
a dream...

Hey! Hey! Hey! Hey!
Look at the sky turn a hell-fire red.
Somebody's house is burning down...
Well, someone stepped from the crowd.
He was nineteen miles high.
He shouts, "We're tired and disgusted,
So we paint red through the sky."

1968

RIOTS

SOVIET TANKS MYLAI
INVADE PRAGUE MASSACRE

EASY RIDER

THESE POWDERS AND PILLS THREATEN OUR NATION'S HEALTH VITALITY AND SELF-RESPECT...

PUEBLO
STUDENT BOBBY
RIOTS KENNEDY
IN PARIS KILLED

L.B.J. CHOOSES NOT TO RUN

So here we are flying
With our heads up in the clouds.
Escaping to the heavens
From the ugly cardboard crowds.
But when will we realize...
That knowing all the time
We must come back down.
And it sure would be a drag to see
The devils still rule our town...
And our freedom...

"...One small step for man,
one giant leap for mankind..."

MUSIC IS STRONGER THAN POLITICS...
IT'S ALWAYS CHANGING ACCORDING TO THE ATTITUDE OF THE PEOPLE, YOU KNOW. WHEN THE
AIR IS STATIC, LOUD AND AGGRESSIVE, THAT'S HOW THE MUSIC GETS. WHEN THE AIR STARTS
GETTIN' PEACEFUL AND HARMONIC AND SO FORTH, THAT'S HOW THE MUSIC WILL GET.

IN THE SPRING OF 1968 I WAS WORKING ON MY NEW ALBUM IN NEW YORK AND DOING A LOT OF JAMMING... I LIKED PLAYING IN REALLY FUNKY, NICE, SWEATY, DIRTY, GRITTY CLUBS... IN NEW YORK YOU MET UP WITH GUYS AND JUST WENT OUT AND JAMMED SOMEWHERE. THE CLUB SCENE WAS SO INFORMAL YOU JUST WENT IN, WAITED YOUR TURN AND GOT UP THERE AND BLEW. IT WAS LIKE A WORKHOUSE. IT WAS NICE TO SWEAT... SOMETIMES EVEN THE GUITARS AND AMPS ACTUALLY SWEATED... THE SWEATIER IT GOT, THE FUNKIER AND GROOVIER.

EVERYBODY MELTED TOGETHER. THE SOUND WAS KICKIN' 'EM ALL IN THE CHEST. I DUG IT.

THAT'S WHAT BEIN' A MUSICIAN IS ALL ABOUT... JAMMING IS KIND OF LIKE MAKING LOVE TO ONE ANOTHER MUSICALLY.

...LIKE MAKING LOVE TO ONE ANOTHER MUSICALLY...

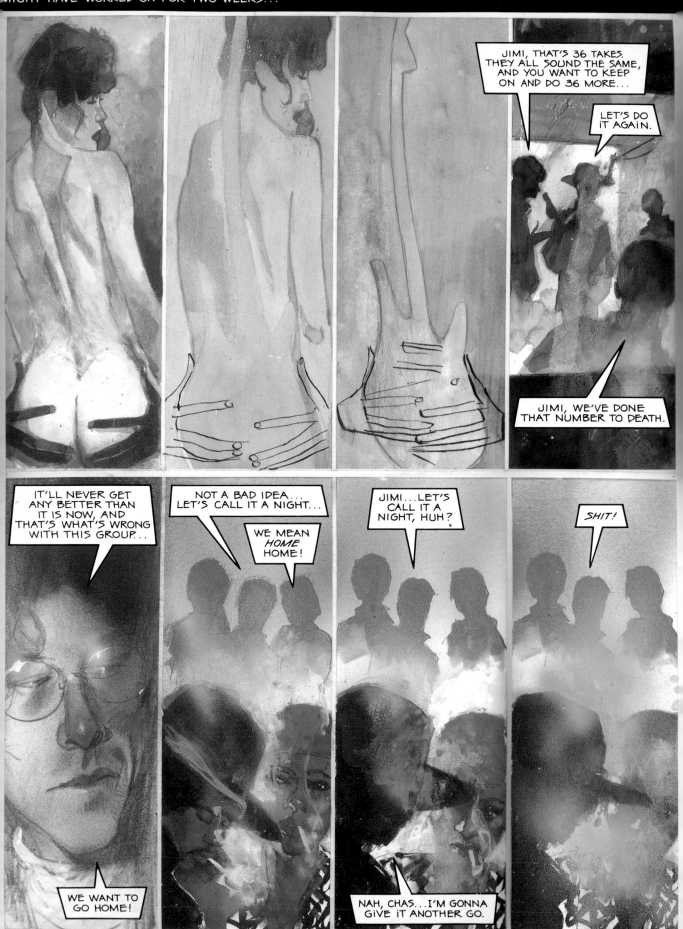

MY OWN THING WAS IN MY HEAD... CHAS WAS GETTIN' REAL UNHAPPY BECAUSE I WASN'T LISTENING TO HIM ANYMORE. WE WERE COMING TO THE END OF OUR JOURNEY... BUT I HEARD THESE SOUNDS, AND I FELT THAT IF I DIDN'T GET THEM TOGETHER, NOBODY ELSE WOULD... I DIDN'T THINK I'D EVER REACH THE POINT WHERE I'D BE SATISFIED, BUT MY ENGINEER, EDDIE KRAMER, WOVE HIS MAGIC, AND I KEPT REACHING FOR IT...

...BESIDES, DEVON ALREADY RENTED IT FOR YOU...

FAR OUT.

SO NOW I HAD TWO NEW PLACES...ONE WAS MY HOME, FULL OF THE MAGIC OF MOROCCO...

...IT WAS LIKE STEPPING INTO ALI BABA'S CAVE...

...AND THE OTHER WAS THE PLACE I BOUGHT TO FULFILL MY DREAM. THE GENERATION CLUB WAS ABOUT TO BE TRANSFORMED INTO ELECTRIC LADY STUDIOS...

THE FUTURE WAS HERE.

UNFORTUNATELY, SO WAS THE PAST.

CAN'T WE DO ANYTHING ABOUT THIS? IT WAS PUT TOGETHER WITH LITTLE BITS OF TAPE THEY USED FROM A JAM SESSION.

DID YOU KNOW IT WAS BEING RECORDED?

JIMI HENDRIX

IT WAS *JUST* A JAM SESSION. HE NEVER TOLD US HE WAS GOING TO RELEASE ANY OF IT...

HE'S ALSO SUING FOR A PIECE OF THE ACTION ON ALL OUR OTHER ALBUMS.

LET HIM SUE. WHAT COURT'S GONNA UPHOLD SOME JIVE PIECE OF PAPER I GOT A DOLLAR FOR A HUNDRED YEARS AGO?

99

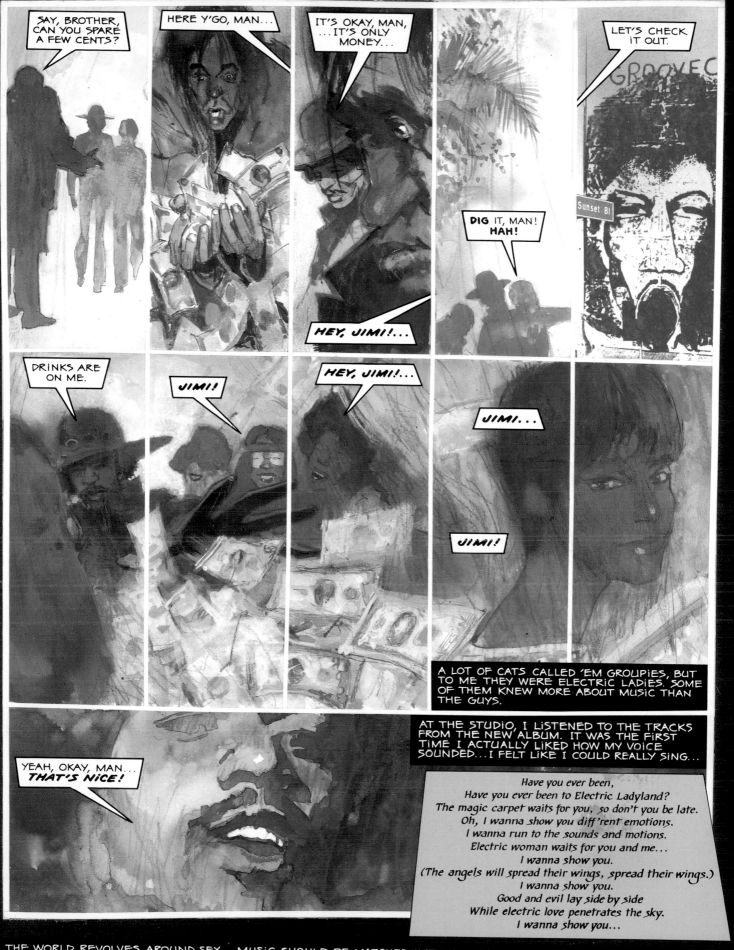

I'D COME TO THE END OF ONE MUSICAL CIRCLE. IT WAS NOW TIME TO GO INTO ANOTHER. THE TROUBLE, THOUGH, WAS PEOPLE WOULDN'T LET ME CHANGE. YOU'RE STILL SUPPOSED TO ENTERTAIN NO MATTER WHAT IS HAPPENING TO YOU AS A MUSICIAN. BUT WHEN YOU GO ONSTAGE AND DO THE SAME OLD THINGS, YOU CAN'T HELP SEEING PEOPLE ARE PUTTING YOU ON... I HAD TO FIND A NEW OUTLET FOR MY MUSIC. I WANTED TO BE PART OF A BIG NEW MUSICAL EXPANSION. THE CIRCLE WAS COMPLETED. IT WAS THE END OF THE BEGINNING — THE START OF SOMETHING ELSE.

GROUP OF THE YEAR

I KNOW YOU GUYS ARE TIRED, BUT RENTING THAT STUDIO 24 HOURS A DAY DIDN'T COME CHEAP. THE LIMOS, THE PARTIES, THE REST OF IT, ALL THAT STUFF HAS TO BE PAID FOR... NOT TO MENTION THE STUDIO YOU'RE BUILDING, JIMI. IT EATS MONEY. BESIDES, YOU WANT THE ALBUM TO BE A HIT, DON'T YOU?

MIAMI
LOS ANGELES
HOUSTON PORTLAND
NEW YORK
NEW HAVEN
BRIDGEPORT
MINNEAPOLIS
SEATTLE
SAN FRANCISCO
CHICAGO
DAVENPORT
PROVIDENCE

I WANTED TO MOVE FURTHER OUT TOWARD A SPIRITUALITY THROUGH MUSIC. WE TRIED TO MAKE OUR MUSIC HIT YOUR SOUL HARD ENOUGH TO MAKE IT OPEN...

#1

INSTRUMENTALIST OF THE WORLD

PERFORMER OF THE YEAR

ELECTRIC LADYLAND

HOLLIES BREAK UP... BLOOD, SWEAT AND TEARS DISBAND. CHAS' CHANDLER LEAVES HENDRIX EXPERIENCE... JIMI HENDRIX GROUP TO SPLIT! (EVERY THREE MONTHS)...

...BUT THE BUSINESS IS RUN BY PEOPLE WHO ONLY THINK ABOUT WHAT IS COMMERCIAL. THE PROMOTERS THINK YOU'RE A MONEY MACHINE. THEY SEE A FAST BUCK AND MAKE YOU A SLAVE TO THE PUBLIC. THEY KEEP YOU AT IT UNTIL YOU'RE EXHAUSTED AND SO IS THE PUBLIC. THAT'S WHY GROUPS BREAK UP — THEY JUST GET WORN OUT.

THE JIMI HENDRIX EXPERIENCE SAVED!

I see hands and tear-stained faces
Reachin' up but not quite touching
the promised land.
Well, I taste tears and a whole lot of
precious years wasted,
Sayin', "Lord, please
give us a helping hand."
Lord, there's got to be some changes.
Gotta be a whole lot of rearranges...

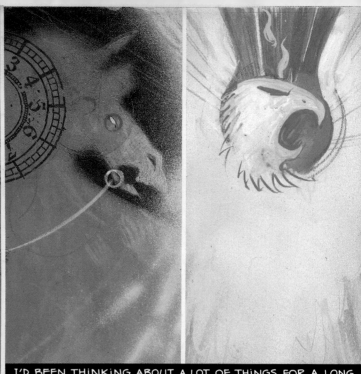

The morning is dead and the day is too. There's nothing left here to greet me but the velvet moon.

All my loneliness I have felt today. It's a little more than enough to make a man throw himself away.

And I continue to burn the midnight lamp, Alone...

YOU ARE NOT ALONE, JIMI...

I'D BEEN THINKING ABOUT A LOT OF THINGS FOR A LONG TIME, AND SUDDENLY IT ALL BECAME VERY CLEAR... IF THERE IS A GOD AND HE MADE YOU, THEN IF YOU BELIEVE IN YOURSELF, YOU'RE ALSO BELIEVING IN HIM. SO I THINK EVERYBODY SHOULD BELIEVE IN HIMSELF: THEN WHAT YOU ARE AND WHAT YOU DO IS YOUR RELIGION. I COULDN'T EXPRESS MYSELF IN EASY CONVERSATION — THE WORDS JUST DIDN'T COME OUT RIGHT. BUT WHEN I GOT UP ON STAGE — WELL, THAT WAS MY WHOLE LIFE. THAT WAS MY RELIGION.

ROYAL ALBERT HALL

MY MUSIC IS ELECTRIC CHURCH MUSIC...

I THINK I'D BETTER HAVE A CHAT WITH HIM AFTER THE SHOW... "ELECTRIC CHURCH," MY ASS...

PURPLE HAZE! FOXY LADY! HEY JOE!

I'M NOT A JUKEBOX!

WE'RE TRYING OUT NEW THINGS...

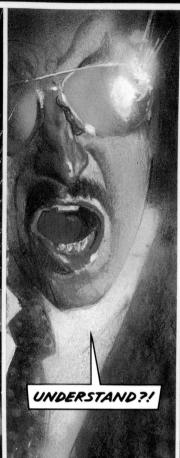

THEY DON'T WANT TO HEAR NEW THINGS!! THEY PAID TO HEAR THEIR OLD FAVORITES! —AND I DON'T WANT TO HEAR ANY MORE SHIT ABOUT THE EXPERIENCE BREAKING UP! I'VE JUST SET UP THE AMERICAN TOUR AND MADE YOU THE HIGHEST PAID ROCK GROUP IN THE WORLD! DON'T SCREW IT UP! GIVE THEM WHAT THEY WANT, OR YOU'LL BLOW IT!

UNDERSTAND?!

YEAH, MIKE... IT'S REAL CLEAR.

MEMPHIS

YEAH, OKAY... OKAY, WE'RE ALL AT CHURCH, ALRIGHT? PRETEND THERE'S A SKY ABOVE YA, ALRIGHT?... GET YOUR HEARTS TOGETHER...

MAN, WAS I HAPPY TO LOOK INTO BILLY COX'S FACE IN THE MIDDLE OF THAT HUGE CROWD. I COULDN'T WAIT TO TALK TO HIM...

I GOT SOMETHING IN MIND I'M WORKING OUT, BILLY... I'LL CALL YOU AS SOON AS I GET THINGS IN PLACE.

MAYBE THE EXPERIENCE COULD HAVE GONE ON, BUT WHAT WOULD HAVE BEEN THE POINT OF THAT?... I WAS INTO NEW THINGS, AND I WANTED TO THINK ABOUT TOMORROW, NOT YESTERDAY... I JUST HOPED THAT MITCH AND NOEL WOULD GET INTO SOMETHING THAT MADE THEM HAPPY...

I MOVED TO THE COUNTRY WITH SOME OF MY OLD PALS, LIKE BILLY COX, BUDDY MILES AND JUMA SULTAN, WHO KNEW ME BEFORE THAT WHOLE STAR TRIP BEGAN...IT WAS GREAT...WE WERE LIKE ONE BIG HAPPY FAMILY, AND I WAS FINALLY ABLE TO GET STARTED WORKING ON SOME NEW SONGS AND ARRANGEMENTS, SO WE'D HAVE SOMETHING NEW TO OFFER...

Meet me in the country.
Meet me in the country.
The city's breath is getting
Way too evil to breathe.
Meet us in the country.
Leave the pigs and rats in the city...
Under the gypsy sun,
We all will clearly reach the grace of living,
To give and receive love with ease.

Oh, strange beautiful grass of green
With your majestic silken scenes.
Your mysterious mountains I wish to see closer.
May I land my kinky machine?

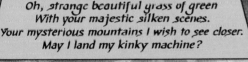

ALL THE THINGS I THOUGHT WERE IMPORTANT BEFORE WERE STILL JUST AS IMPORTANT. TRYING TO UNDERSTAND PEOPLE AND RESPECT THEIR FEELINGS REGARDLESS OF THEIR POSITION OR YOURS.

THE BEAUTIFUL THINGS WERE STILL THE SAME — THE SUNSET AND THE DEW ON THE GRASS. IF YOU'RE LOOKING FOR REAL HAPPINESS, YOU GO BACK TO THE HAPPIEST DAYS YOU HAD AS A CHILD. REMEMBER WHEN PLAYING IN THE RAIN WAS FUN?

500,000 Halos...
Outshined the mud and history.
We washed and drank in
God's tears of joy,
And for once...And for everyone—
The truth was not a mystery—
Love called to all...Music is Magic.
As we passed over and beyond the walls of Nay
Hand in hand as we lived and
Made real the dreams of peaceful men—
We came together...danced with
The pearls of rainy weather
Riding the Waves of Music and Space...
Music is Magic...
Magic is Life...
Love as never loved before...
Harmony to Son and Daughter...
Man and Wife...

...AND SO WAS MY DISCUSSION WITH MIKE BACK AT THE STUDIO...

OH...THIS IS JUST *GREAT*, JIMI!

YOU PLAY WITH THIS *NOWHERE* GYPSY BAND, AND I GOT WARNERS AND TRACK SCREAMING AT ME! WE *STILL* OWE AN ALBUM!!

SHIT!... AND HERE ARE YOUR COURT PAPERS! A TRIAL DATE'S BEEN *SET!*

SOME PEOPLE SAID, "HE PLAYS WHITE ROCK FOR WHITE PEOPLE. WHAT'S HE DOING HERE?" I DIDN'T LOOK AT THINGS IN TERMS OF RACE. THE ESTABLISHMENT WAS TRYING TO SELL THAT, BUT IT WAS REALLY BETWEEN THE OLD AND THE NEW. I WANTED TO SHOW THAT MUSIC IS UNIVERSAL. BESIDES, SOME OF THOSE KIDS DIDN'T HAVE SIX DOLLARS TO GO TO MADISON SQUARE GARDEN.

HARLEM STREET FAIR

HEY, BROTHER, YOU BETTER COME **HOME**.

I FELT A PART OF WHAT THE PANTHERS WERE DOING, BUT NOT FOR THE AGGRESSION OR VIOLENCE. I'M NOT FOR GUERRILLA WARFARE. I WISH THEY'D HAD ELECTRIC GUITARS IN THE COTTON FIELDS. A WHOLE LOT OF THINGS WOULD HAVE BEEN STRAIGHTENED OUT. NOT JUST FOR BLACK AND WHITE BUT FOR THE CAUSE.

WELL, *YOU* GOTTA DO WHAT *YOU* GOTTA DO, AND *I* GOTTA DO WHAT *I* GOTTA DO.

115

BILLY, BUDDY AND I DID A GIG FOR BILL GRAHAM. THE BAND OF GYPSYS HIT THE FILLMORE EAST...

THIS NEXT SONG IS DEDICATED TO ALL THE TROOPS IN HARLEM, CHICAGO, AND, OH YES... VIETNAM...

*Machine Gun tearin'
my body all apart.
Machine Gun tearin'
my body all apart.
Evil man
make me kill you.
Evil man
make you kill me.
Evil man
make me kill you...
Even though we're only
families apart...*

I **NEED** YOU, GODDAMIT! WILL YOU **STOP** WITH THOSE **TAPES**?!

THIS IS WHAT I **DO**, MIKE... OR DID YOU FORGET?

AND **THIS IS** WHAT **I** DO. THE ALBUM YOU'RE SO BUSY PERFECTING GOES TO PAY OFF THAT HALF-ASSED CONTRACT YOU WERE DUMB ENOUGH TO SIGN FOR A **DOLLAR**!

WE DON'T GET **SQUAT**, SO **SCREW IT**!

NOW I NEED YOUR SIGNATURE **HERE**!

CONTRACT

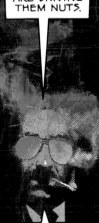

??!... I GOTTA SIGN A NOTE FOR **ANOTHER** $350,000, AND THE STUDIO'S IN **YOUR** NAME?

JIMI...JIMI... WE'VE BEEN **THROUGH** ALL THAT. THE F.B.I.'S WATCHING YOU BECAUSE THE KIDS ALL LOVE YOU, AND THE KIDS ARE DRIVING THEM NUTS.

BAD GUYS DO A LOT OF BUSINESS DOWN HERE, AND THEY DON'T LIKE ALL THE ATTENTION YOU'RE GETTING FROM THE FEDS.

...I'M JUST TRYING TO **PROTECT** YOU, JIMI...

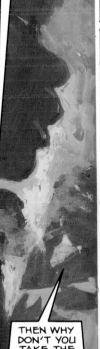

THEN WHY DON'T YOU TAKE THE BREAD FROM THE EUROPEAN ROYALTIES?

BECAUSE THE ROYALTIES ARE ALL BEING HELD. WE ARE BEING SUED THERE UNDER THE SAME CONTRACT!

IN **OTHER** WORDS, JIMI...

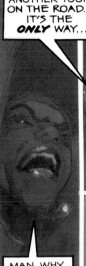

...**THERE AIN'T NO BREAD!**

...**THAT'S** WHY I WANT TO GET THE **EXPERIENCE** BACK TOGETHER AND PUT ANOTHER TOUR ON THE ROAD... IT'S THE **ONLY** WAY...

MAN, WHY DON'T YOU JUST GET THE FUCK OUT OF HIS **FACE** AND LEAVE HIM **ALONE**!?

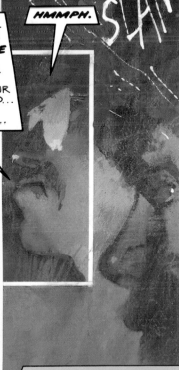

HMMPH.

*Don't you come no closer.
The path is gettin' colder.
Get away from my door,
Unless you want to start another war.*

117

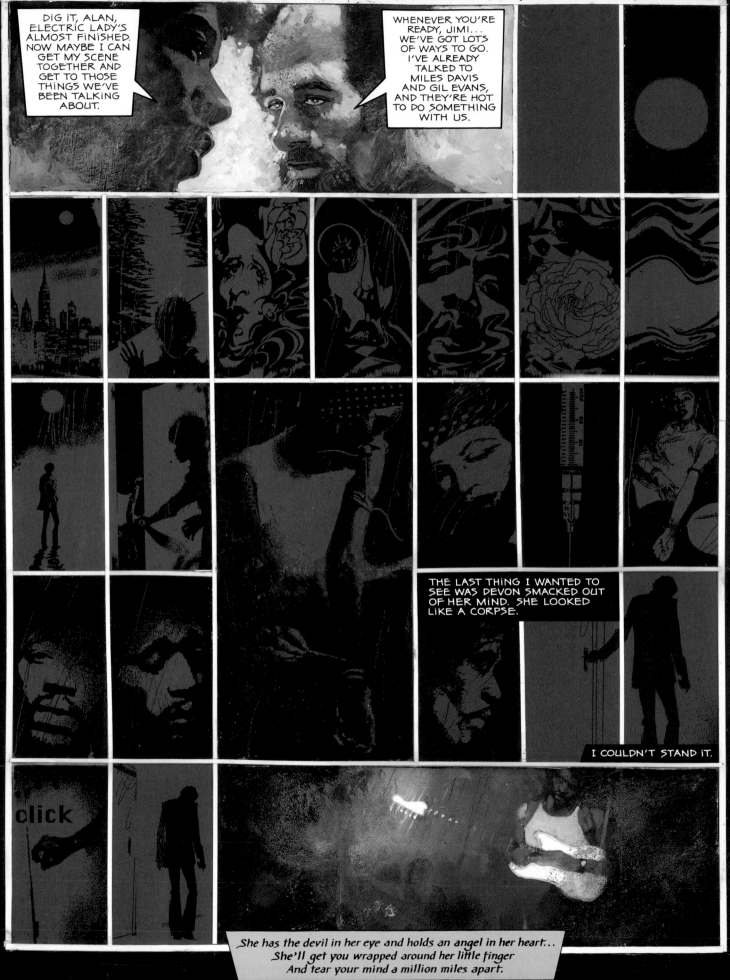

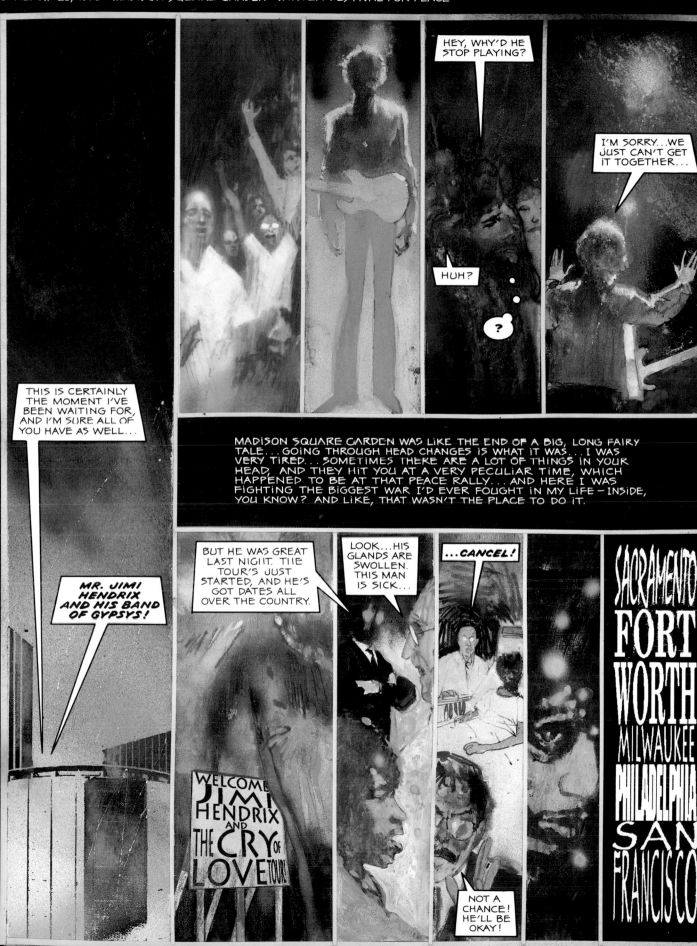

MAY 30, 1970 · BERKELEY COMMUNITY THEATER
BERKELEY, CALIFORNIA

Oh, say, can you see it's really
such a mess.
Every inch of earth is a
fighting nest.
Giant pencil and lipstick tube
shaped things
Continue to rain and cause
screaming pain.
And the Arctic stains from
silver blue to bloody red...

...Forget about the past, baby.
Things ain't what they
used to be...
They say, "Power to the people."
That's what they're screamin' —
Freedom of the soul.
Pass it on, pass it on to
the young and old.

AUGUST 26, 1970
ELECTRIC LADY STUDIOS
OPENING PARTY

NOW I CAN START MY
ELECTRIC CHURCH
CARAVAN. I KNOW
WE CAN DO IT. IT'S
GONNA BE ALRIGHT...
SOON AS I GET BACK
FROM THE ROAD.

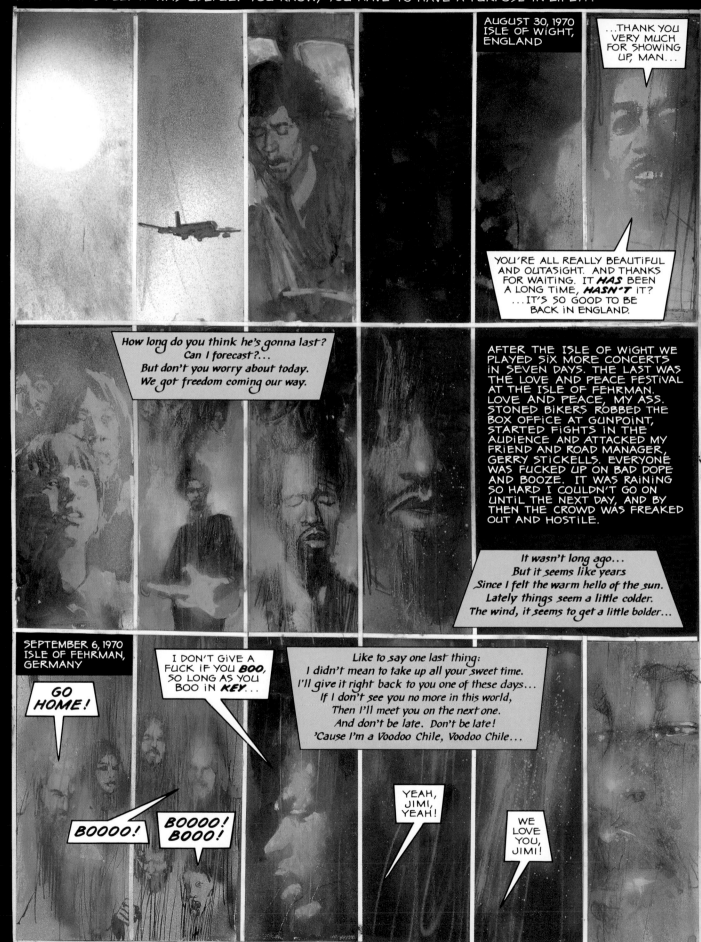

AUGUST 30, 1970
ISLE OF WIGHT,
ENGLAND

...THANK YOU VERY MUCH FOR SHOWING UP, MAN...

YOU'RE ALL REALLY BEAUTIFUL AND OUTASIGHT. AND THANKS FOR WAITING. IT **HAS** BEEN A LONG TIME, **HASN'T** IT? ...IT'S SO GOOD TO BE BACK IN ENGLAND.

How long do you think he's gonna last?
Can I forecast?...
But don't you worry about today.
We got freedom coming our way.

AFTER THE ISLE OF WIGHT WE PLAYED SIX MORE CONCERTS IN SEVEN DAYS. THE LAST WAS THE LOVE AND PEACE FESTIVAL AT THE ISLE OF FEHRMAN. LOVE AND PEACE, MY ASS. STONED BIKERS ROBBED THE BOX OFFICE AT GUNPOINT, STARTED FIGHTS IN THE AUDIENCE AND ATTACKED MY FRIEND AND ROAD MANAGER, GERRY STICKELLS. EVERYONE WAS FUCKED UP ON BAD DOPE AND BOOZE. IT WAS RAINING SO HARD I COULDN'T GO ON UNTIL THE NEXT DAY, AND BY THEN THE CROWD WAS FREAKED OUT AND HOSTILE.

It wasn't long ago...
But it seems like years
Since I felt the warm hello of the sun.
Lately things seem a little colder.
The wind, it seems to get a little bolder...

SEPTEMBER 6, 1970
ISLE OF FEHRMAN,
GERMANY

GO HOME!

I DON'T GIVE A FUCK IF YOU **BOO**, SO LONG AS YOU BOO IN **KEY**...

Like to say one last thing:
I didn't mean to take up all your sweet time.
I'll give it right back to you one of these days...
If I don't see you no more in this world,
Then I'll meet you on the next one.
And don't be late. Don't be late!
'Cause I'm a Voodoo Chile, Voodoo Chile...

BOOOO!

BOOOO! BOOO!

YEAH, JIMI, YEAH!

WE LOVE YOU, JIMI!

BY THE TIME I GOT BACK TO ENGLAND I WAS REALLY WIPED OUT, BUT I WAS BUZZING WITH LOTS OF NEW IDEAS AND PLANS. THERE'S NO PLACE LIKE LONDON, AND THAT'S WHERE I THOUGHT I'D GET IT ALL TOGETHER — JUST LIKE THE FIRST TIME.

IT'S REALLY GOOD TO SEE YOU AGAIN, CHAS. I'D LIKE YOU TO LISTEN TO THE MUSIC I'VE BEEN LAYING DOWN.

...AND MY GIRLFRIEND, MONIKA DANNEMANN.

Hello, my friend.
So good to see you again.
I've been all by myself.
I don't think I can make it alone.
I gotta keep pushing ahead.

IT WAS GREAT JAMMING AGAIN AT RONNIE SCOTT'S CLUB, AND HANGING OUT WITH GOOD FRIENDS LIKE ALAN, STELLA, ERIC BURDON...

DON'T WORRY, MAN, WE'LL STRAIGHTEN OUT ALL THE HASSLES.

I HOPE SO.

SURE, JIMI...I'D BE GLAD TO. BRING THE TAPES BACK FROM NEW YORK, AND WE'LL GO THROUGH THEM HERE...AWAY FROM EVERYONE.

...It seems we've been walking
For a thousand miles
To a destination
That escaped my memory...

Freedom!
That's what I want now.
Freedom!
That's what I need now.
Freedom to live.
Freedom so I can give.

JUST ONE MORE SHOT, MONIKA... JUST ONE MORE.

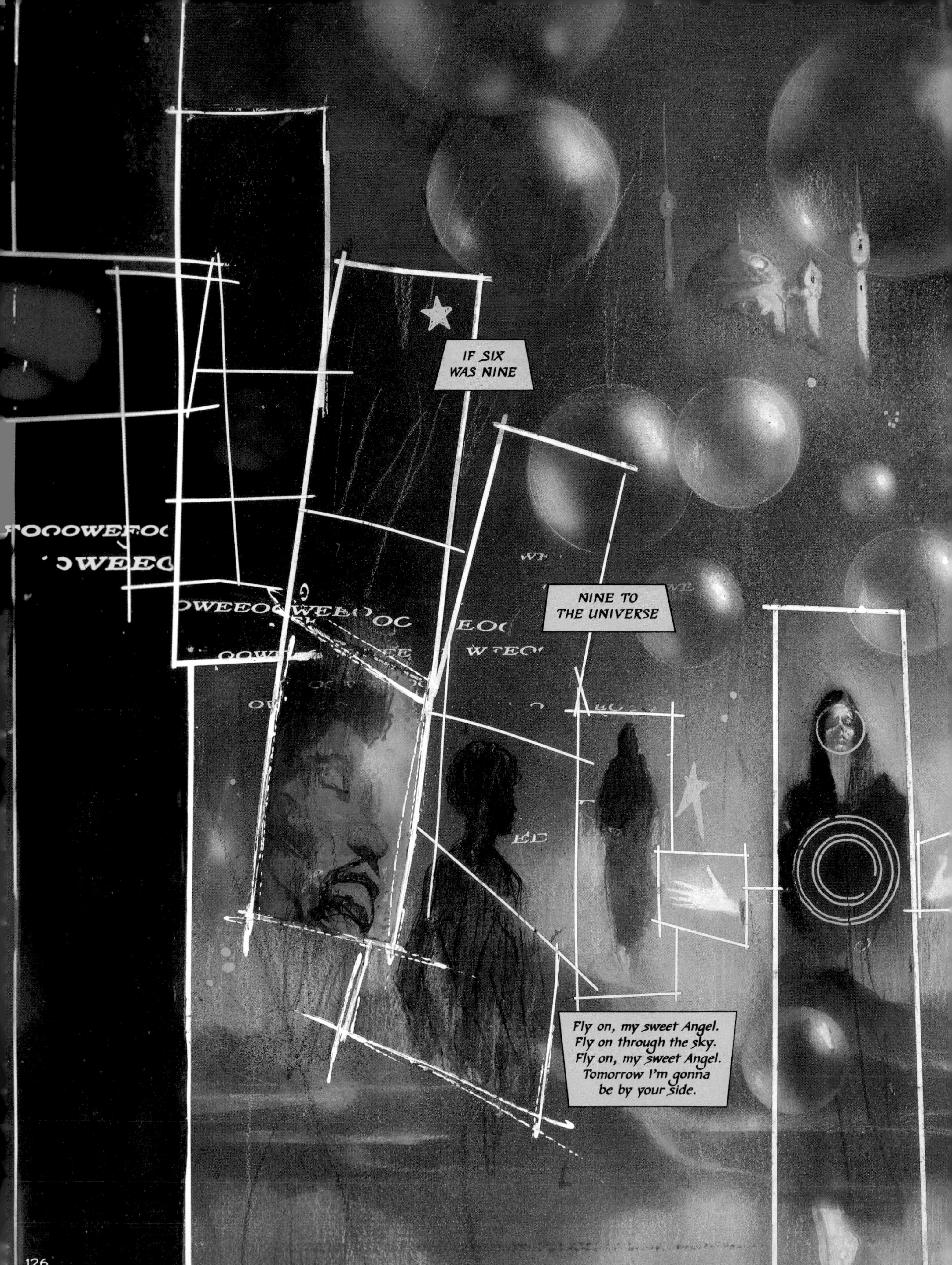
IF SIX WAS NINE
NINE TO THE UNIVERSE
Fly on, my sweet Angel. Fly on through the sky. Fly on, my sweet Angel. Tomorrow I'm gonna be by your side.

NOW

It's Time, JIMI

It's TIME

Sure enough this mornin' came unto me,
Silver wings silhouette against a child's sunrise.
And my Angel, she said unto me,
"Today is the day for you to rise…"

If I don't see you no more in this world
Then I'll meet you on the next one.
And don't be late. Don't be late!
'Cause I'm a Voodoo Chile, Voodoo Chile.
Lord knows I'm a Voodoo Chile!

ROCK IDOL JIMI HENDRIX
DIED IN LONDON TODAY.
HENDRIX, CONSIDERED BY
MANY TO HAVE BEEN
THE GREATEST GUITARIST
THAT EVER LIVED, WAS
27 YEARS OLD…
HE CHANGED THE FACE OF…

the Story
of life is quicker
than the wink of an eye.
the story
of love is hello
and goodbye...
until we meet again.